LORE OF WOLVERINE COUNTRY

by

STAN PERKINS

BROADBLADE PRESS
11314 Miller Road
Swartz Creek, MI 48473

Typeset and printed in the United States of America
Sans Serif, Inc., and McNaughton & Gunn.

MAR '87

DEDICATED TO THE WOLVERINE

HISTORY RECORDS that the entire heavily timbered Great Lakes Basin was the habitat of this cunning carnivorous mammal. He resembled a small bear in many of his physical characteristics and was seldom caught in a trap. He was a mischievous nocturnal traveler that would break into camps and cabins and consume all the edibles he could find. This beast would also snitch small movable items that he had absolutely no use for and conceal them for personal admiration at a later time. A wolverine would cap off a raid by spraying the premises with a vile smelling secretion that was the trademark of the species.

This Gulo luscus is crafty and very intelligent. He is a joker. I am using the wolverine as a symbolic figurehead for this book because his character fits its intent.

It is with remorse, I would add, that this fearless voracious animal is thought to be extinct in the Great Lakes Watershed. After considerable painstaking research there remains a faint ray of hope that a few pair may still be propagating their kind in some remote depths of the Canadian Wilderness.

If a miracle should come to pass, the wolverine may stage a comeback and become numerous once again with assistance from environmental and conservation organizations. Homo sapiens needs a resurgence of the quality of competition which only the Gulo luscus can craftily provide.

ACKNOWLEDGEMENTS

Maude Baker
Dean Bawks
Terry Cousineau and Sons
Myrtle R. Elie
Richard and Ellen Kaiser
Claude Mundy
Victor Nash

George and Hila O'Brien
Thomas W. Perkins
Frank Robinson
David Scheidemantel
Nelson Gerald Scott
Mildred Smith
Duane Upton

Edited by
Mary J. Shaw

CONTENTS

LIST OF
ILLUSTRATIONS

PROLOGUE

HAVING BEEN BLESSED by creation with the largest supply of fresh water in the known universe, rich soil, great forests, valuable deposits of minerals and other natural resources, the Great Lakes Watershed has long served as a haven for a relaxed people. For generations, peace loving inhabitants of both the United States and Canada have shared this space as beneficiaries. It was endowed by nature to provide a substantial living for all those who desired to avail themselves of it since the first adventurers of the day, "coureurs de bois," traversed the territory. Michigan, the Wolverine State, is the axis of the area.

This atmosphere lends to the making of a contented and happy people. Exuberant people are a relaxed people. They recall events and retell them as stories, usually with exaggerations. They relate incidents, fabrications, prevarications and plain bold-faced lies for the fun of it. This is a normal characteristic of the people.

The scope of this informative folklore and humor is boundless. Ethnic backgrounds, occupations and diversified recreational interests of the people who live about the Great Lakes provide a voluminous source. For example — it can include pranks perpetrated upon a factory production worker. By following industrial employment backward to its fountainhead, one uncovers the personnel of the supporting cast as the steel-mill worker, the trucker, the sailor, the miner, etc.

The same is true of agriculture. If we run it backward to the days of the pioneers, a wealth of anecdotes and amusing lore comes to light.

Yet another large business of the area is the tourist trade. It presently covers the so-called resort business that provides all the comforts of home while away from home. This is a complete reversal from the status of the early voyageurs who lived out-of-doors without any of the amenities of today's campers.

A couple of hundred years ago when one went off into the wilds he was taking his life in his own hands. This leads off into the forest and the unknown for the yarns of the fisherman, hunter, trapper and lumberman.

Truly, the base for these sketches is without restriction and the material unlimited. In spite of the vast amount of material available, this book is restricted to hearsay, personal experiences and public occurrences that were not far removed from the life style of the author.

The personal intent is to bring forward and preserve a bit of the brighter, the lighter, the rollicking side of life as enjoyed by these fabulous people who reside in the vicinity of the Great Lakes Basin. I have attempted to lend depth and to justify these descriptive literary sketches by infusing an educational infrastructure.

Stanley Cozadd Perkins

CHAPTER I

SAGA OF THE COUNTRY SCHOOL

IN THE DAYS of the one-room country school, boys were boys and sometimes the girls tried to be. Out there, the mischievous innocence of the country youth would often nurture the need for immediate corrective action by the teacher and sometimes the school board. Pity the youngster who did not toe the line and especially the one whose dad was on the school board. The teacher was always right. As soon as his parents heard about him getting a licking from the teacher (and the bad news would always beat him home), there would be a second one waiting in the woodshed. Some of the "carryings on" that precipitated this severe chastisement have been mellowed by time. Their recalling brings forth a smile, a chuckle and a myriad of humorous reflections the likes of which I will attempt to reiterate.

Turbulence was also generated, in the institution called the one-room school, by individuals and between individuals. The volunteers contained few "students" and for that reason were usually referred to as "pupils." I use the word volunteers because, for most of that period in our history, education was not compulsory. Book learning was assimilated only when it was convenient for the "assimilee" to do so. This pertained to all of the boys over

1

The
One
Room
School...

The bell no longer rings its
   call to start the class,
The windows all are boarded,
   up that once held glass.

The pump no longer works,
   it's lost its prime,
And boards once painted
   red, show only grime.

But listen, listen closely,
   can't you hear,
The echo of young voices,
   from a far off year.

Or is that echo merely
   in my mind?
Of sounds remembered,
   back in childhood's time?

By Maude Baker

ONE-ROOM SCHOOL

twelve years and to a few of the older girls whose services were also required at home. The period of time when they did attend the one-room country school was suitably named the winter term. It ran until spring breakup. This split the country school year into three sessions, now called semesters, with the winter term being the best attended and most interesting.

The fall session would begin soon after Labor Day which was no holiday in the country, because as they used to say, "every day is labor day." The fall term would allow a young or new teacher time to get her feet on the ground, become acquainted with the families in her district, and to spend extra effort with the new, timid and frightened first graders. There was no such thing as the kindergarten. Kindergarten was spent at home on the mother's knee where the child was taught numbers and letters. The teacher picked it up from there.

Pristine Education

When the young teacher took over in the fall session she inherited problems that were not academic. It was the social outlook of the fledgling that was upsetting. All at once he was thrust into a foreign world; he had to be domesticated. Since birth, he would be lucky if he had seen few other humans besides his own immediate family, and then only slyly by peering at them with his finger in his mouth and his head hung low from behind his mother's voluminous petticoats. He was backward and shy. As long as his mind remained in this recessive condition the darndest things could happen. It was up to the young teacher to snap him out of it before the winter term began and the boisterous older pupils descended from the harvest fields like a flock of noisy blackbirds to the quiet country schoolhouse.

This beginner reacted to association with strangers much as a fawn would if taken away from the doe in the surrounding forest. His folks would try their best to prepare him for this change of environment by talking with him about it during the preceding summer. However, many times the parents themselves were a backward lot and of little assistance.

So for many youngsters, the first grade at the one-room country school was traumatic. The first order of business was getting them to the schoolhouse — and on time. I recall a kid who would go down the dirt road about forty rods (he had to walk two miles) and stand in the middle of the road and bellow. Next he would start to jump up and down in protest against going further down the road — until his father would come up onto the roadway with a goodly section of willow, then he would begin moving in the direction of the classes of the morning in great haste. Another boy would not go to school unless a large neighbor boy carried him on his back. The little girls were much less trouble. They would mind their mothers. It was said that good manners made a man out of a boy, but little girls were made of "sugar and spice and everything nice" and they were no trouble at all.

Once this new first grade boy was in the school yard the troubles were just beginning. The teacher, with the help of other pupils could usually get him inside, especially if it was windy or raining.

I was told about a backwoods boy who once in the schoolhouse could not be cajoled or threatened into removing his hat and coat and taking a seat. He stood in the back of the room first on one foot, then the other, until dinnertime. He would eat the contents of his dinner pail which consisted of cold buttermilk pancakes and take off for home on a dead run. The young teacher put up with his shenanigans until late one morning while he was standing in the back of the room, he wet his pants. The wide, old, pegged pine boards in the schoolhouse floor were hollowed out and tilted toward the teacher's desk. This was the last straw. She put a note in the boy's dinner bucket asking his folks to keep him at home until the spring term because she did not think her school was ready for their son yet.

Another pronounced problem with these boys that were products of backwoods families was today what we define as discipline. In those times it was called making them mind. Actually it was the process of rearranging the pupils' minds so they were compatible with the teacher's mind. Her mind was in a way related to the mood she was in. Regardless, the teacher had to get their attention. When all else failed, she went to her "no no" cabinet under the world map case and brought out a "cat-o'-three-tails." It was a short piece of broken mop handle with three pieces of rawhide attached that would sting through your pants and heavy underwear like "old Friday." The school board members had fixed it up for her and also had given her the authority to use it as needed. It was used sparingly on first graders, but just the threat of the weapon and the knowledge that it was there and available made it her number-one attention getter. There was the problem of making a pupil sit at the desk that he was assigned to and making him be quiet. These pupils were fresh out of the brush and were used to running around like coyote pups and yipping at about the same speed. It was difficult to make them understand that order must be kept so that the other seven grades could be taught. Everyone had to sit down, shut up and stay put. This was called keeping order.

Once the teacher had this into their wild little heads, she was beginning to break them to school as one would a mustang to respect the halter. Much like a wild colt, some of them would balk.

A story came out of the woods concerning a man who developed into a leader in his community, who had spent his first year in the country school without uttering one word. He was balky. During the recesses and the noon hour he played and talked with the other children in a normal way, but once the bell rang and order was called, nary a word would escape his lips. Of course, he was not allowed to pass the first grade. When school was called for the fall session the next year, he was seated with a new set of first graders. This evidently made him mad. His pride was on the line as he blurted out, "I am not going to sit with those little kids."

The spell of silence was broken and as a reward he was then and there promoted to the second grade.

Conflict Between the Sexes

The school desks were constructed with a built-in inkwell. Pencils as we know them today were nonexistent. Writing was done with chalk on individual slates or on the wall-blackboards and by pen and ink. Inkwells were the source of much trouble for the teacher, either accidental or intentional.

There was a strong saucy fifth-grade girl who delighted in tantalizing the freckle-faced boy in the desk behind. Her favorite maneuver was to tilt her head back and turn it briskly from side to side so that her large light brown braid of hair would sweep his desk clean at a time when he was the least prepared to protect it. His composition book, tablet, loose papers, pen, slate pencil and whatever, would go a flying. The teacher never seemed to catch on; so the freckle-faced boy decided to do his own rectifying. "An eye for an eye and a tooth for a tooth," he remembered the preacher reading from the Good Book. The end of her pigtail was laying over on his desk one day instead of down her back where it belonged. It appeared to him as though she was getting into position to pull off another of her swishing antics. Gently he lifted the end of her pigtail and inserted it into his inkwell. Her soft hair took up the dark blue ink like a sponge. Almost immediately school was excused for recess. The freckle-faced one took off for the schoolhouse door and the usual scrub ball game. He was saved by the bell. He was outdoors and in the clear.

After recess when school was called back to order the results were as follows. His desk was well smeared. Her dress was a mess and the pigtail well-dyed. The teacher called it an accident which "we will have to take care to see that it does not happen again." It was the end of all of her pigtail swishing antics.

The Fire Builder

Thanksgiving was no big holiday at the country school except for a little gobbling around. When school was called to order

PIGTAIL SWISHERS AND SCHOOLHOUSE PRIVY
Photographs courtesy of Crossroads Village and the Huckleberry Railroad.

after the two-day Thanksgiving recess it brought on the winter term. It was a challenge to the teacher and a whole new ball game because of the increased enrollment of those older young people fresh from the harvest fields.

Once upon a time there was a country schoolboy who was very happy with his personal lot. Life for him was just fine. It could not have been better. He liked his teacher and the other pupils in the school. On the spur of the moment he decided to be a do-gooder.

It was a snappy December Monday morning. He decided to do something unusual at the school and it turned out exactly that way.

Custom and the terms of her contract decreed that the teacher arrive a half hour before classes were scheduled to begin, kindle a fire in the old potbellied wood heater and have the chill off the room, somewhat, by the time she rang the last bell. This perpetrator came up with the idea that he would get to school about an hour early (the door was never locked), build the fire and have it all warm and cozy by the time anyone else showed up.

The stove was in the middle of a large rectangular room entirely surrounded by wood; the floor, the side walls and ceiling. In addition there were flimsy curtains, window shades, and crepe paper Christmas decorations draped everywhere. Into the potbellied stove went kindling and split dry hardwood, crammed as high as the top of the stove door; a couple sheets of a Roebuck Catalog were tucked in between the sticks, along with a dash of coal oil. The soft glow of one match sent the whole pile rushing up the tin stovepipe. This stovepipe was in thirty-inch lengths. It was suspended only by wire for a space of thirty feet from the center of the room to the chimney, which stood outside the north wall. The steel sides of the stove began to glow in various shades of red.

The do-gooder basked in this new warmth with his backside toward the stove, contemplating the surprise and appreciation of the teacher and his classmates as they burst through the door into a warm room for a change. His ears picked up at the sound of an unfamiliar noise. Before he could turn to close the draft it had changed to a roar. Looking toward the noise, he noticed the tin stovepipe was also glowing and the crepe paper ribbons hanging below it were losing their elasticity. Soon he could smell the heat scorching the painted ceiling. The chimney was burning out. It was just like a blow torch. Would the schoolhouse burn? Out-of-doors he went for a look-see. Flames were shooting ten feet high out from the top of the chimney. Soot and black smoke were blanketing the vicinity. Joe Ringlein and his son Bert saw it from their horse stable door and they came over, from close by, on the run.

Their quick appraisal was that, "She may go. If fire breaks out above that red hot pipe in the ceiling, there is little we can do to save her. It does not look good right now. Let's clean out the schoolhouse."

A window was opened. Every last object that was not nailed down was passed out the window and placed in a pile in the schoolyard at a safe distance from the hot building. The library books, maps, teaching supplies, the teacher's desk drawers with contents intact and everything in each pupil's desk were all removed. About the time the clean-out was completed, the teacher arrived followed shortly by the do-gooder's schoolmates.

The creosote and soot in the red hot stovepipe and chimney soon burnt themselves out. Joe and Bert Ringlein returned to their barn across the road.

They did not say much except, "That chimney had to burn out sometime."

School classes started an hour late that day. Everything was so disorganized that it took a lot of sorting to get all the stuff in the yard back where it belonged. Very little learning took place because of the confusion.

Before final dismissal at four, the teacher asked the fire builder to remain seated and for all the rest to get on their coats and to leave promptly, which they appeared to do.

After a lengthy lecture the teacher went to her wall cabinet and took out the "cat-o'-three-tails." She waltzed the guilty one around the now cold potbellied stove five times. Once for each day of the school week with a healthy swat each time he passed the stove door to remind him never to start a fire in that stove again. There were some whines, squeals and yells, more from hurt feelings than anything else, but the worst hurt came when he heard the laughing pupils outside the door. They did not leave the school yard when dismissed but instead hung around to cash in on the excitement. The news of the very hot schoolhouse stove had beat the do-gooder home. His supper did not go down easily or taste too good. Afterward his dad invited him out to the wood-shed. Dad understood like only dads do.

"Shucks son, any chimney has to burn itself out sometime. You weren't to blame and were only trying to help. Let's get together on this thing. I will pound on the door here a couple of times, you give a yell and we will go back into the house. It's cold and drafty out here. The womenfolk will never know the difference." This kind of conniving builds strong bonds between fathers and sons.

Stuck in the Culvert

A country school was usually located on one acre of ground. You as a pupil were not supposed to leave that school yard during school hours without the teacher's permission. There were the out buildings where you could play "anty-I-over," a small ball dia-mond, some poison ivy hanging on the line fence, a few trees to climb, the well pump and perhaps one good mud hole. That was about it. For ten to twenty active growing kids, it was confining. At home they pretty much roamed at will through farm build-ings, fields and woods, not only their own, but those of the neigh-bors.

Under the side dirt road adjacent to the school grounds was an eighteen inch concrete culvert put there years before for drainage purposes. The boys got to playing around the culvert. They rolled balls through and got sticks to poke them out when they did not go all the way. Next they crawled in to get the ball. It was fun inside the culvert, especially when a team and wagon rumbled over the topside. They would even eat their lunches in there stretched out head to toe. The teacher did not object, thinking it was only a passing fancy and they only played there when it was dry. As the days grew shorter the boys wore more clothing includ-ing heavy mackinaw jackets. The six foot sections of the culvert

IMPORTANT OUTBUILDINGS
A portion of the Ryno School yard in Clayton Township, Genesee County, Michigan showing the woodshed and the boys' outhouse. This woodshed also served as a daytime stable for the teacher's driving horse. Date; Spring of 1919.

were not perfectly aligned and there was one place near the middle of the road where it was a tight squeeze for the largest boy.

One late fall day when the pupils were called back in after the noon recess, there was an empty seat. It was supposed to be filled by an eighth grade boy.

"Where is Chester?" asked the teacher. Immediately they all knew. A distressed howl that sounded like it was coming from a lost coyote pup pierced the air. Chet was stuck in the culvert. That was the end of classes for that afternoon. The whole school went out to the side road. The teacher put a couple of the small boys in the hole fore and aft to pull and push in unison on the big boy to try to chuck him out of there. No avail; the boys were not strong enough. He could move a bit, but his heavy mackinaw jacket would not. He could not get his arms out of the sleeves. Chet was like an unshucked peanut. He could be chucked back and forth a wee bit, but not released. The boy, large as he was, lost his composure after the two small boys gave up. He began to cry and yell. He was panic-stricken in short order.

The school had no phone, and the nearest one was like a half mile away. There was no such organization as a rescue unit in those days. No, not even a volunteer fire department. The teacher had to get to that phone. Away she went on a run. To call whom? The best person, she decided, would be the school board moderator. Before long, all three members of the board were on the side road trying to get relief to the screaming eighth grader. They pushed a rope in to him with a stick. He held on while the three of them pulled. The trouble was the boy did not have strength enough left to hold on. They tried the other end. A small boy went into the culvert with the rope and tied it around his shoes. The three men pulled. A crowd was gathering. Everyone that happened to be passing on either road stopped with advice. The party line telephone was also spreading the word.

By tying a rope to his feet and shoes, several men pulled him about a foot but the heavy coat slid up towards his chest and neck like a tightening wedge. The coat was choking him as the boy continued to carry on more than ever, because his parents had now arrived at the scene. His father took charge.

"That is my boy down there. We are going to dig him out. Go get a team, a plow and a shovel for every man." The dirt road was as hard as cement, but they did plow about half way down to the culvert. It was only two feet below road level.

The dirt flew off the shovels for less than ten minutes before they lifted out the section of culvert immediately in front of his sobbing face. Strong gentle hands slid him forward and up from the hole. He did not seem to be in too tight. The fact was, he had just given up from trying. He had trouble standing erect for a while but soon regained his composure. The local populace arose to the occasion.

There were some repercussions for the teacher. Her contract was not renewed. All the boys had to take a trip to the woodshed with their dads. No one at that school crawled under the road again. But the memories that stuck around were humorous. Chubby Chet was the butt of all kinds of jokes for years. The ribbing he was forced to endure was not about becoming stuck in the tile as most people surmised. It was a horse of a different color that only a few close schoolmates were in on. Chet was so scared about the whipping that he knew awaited him in the woodshed at home, that he mussed his britches.

Straw Stack Love

At another country school a straw stack from the threshing machine was blown right up close to the school yard fence. In fact, some of it sloped over into the yard on the backside. Youngsters were used to straw. They all handled it, jumped in it and played in it at home. They proceeded to gang up on this particular stack. They burrowed through and under it like a pack of woodchucks until the entire stack was a maze of crawlable tunnels. It was used both by the boys and the girls and together. It became an extracurricular course held at recess time for exploratory purposes. The writer has attended a few school reunions for this particular institution of lower learning, just as an observer. I have come to the conclusion that there will be no end to the jests, jokes and stories based on the tunnelled straw stack and the self-taught sex education classes held there, until all those that participated are six foot under. It has been told that one Saturday night some parents touched a match to this memorable straw stack because they calculated that it was the proper thing to do. It smoldered for a week, but I have heard that fires kindled within pupils of that particular country school under that stack are still smoldering.

Iced Outhouse

No season of the year was exempt from pranks and deviltry around a one-room school. In winter time, ice and snow were the vehicles. Sometimes the yard would be rolled clean of snow in the building of snowmen, forts, etc. Boys are naturally born aggres-

STRAW STACK MAKER
Photo by A. M. Wettach

sive. They explore possibilities. In this case it was during the afternoon recess.

"Let's roll some of this soft snow into the boy's privy. It would plug up some of the cracks and make it warmer." So it was agreed. They went to work like only boys can when they want to, but they went too far. They filled their outhouse with wet snow right to the eaves. To complete the job, they stood back and fired wet snowballs into the vent near the peak even though the vent was not needed.

Recess was over. The bell rang. At four o'clock they were dismissed for the day. All went home without another thought about their snow filled outhouse. The rascals!

That night the heavy wet snow ceased to be. The sky cleared off from the north. In the morning the air was crisp and clear. The thermometer said nothing. Exactly zero was the reading. It was school as usual. Before the last bell rang, one of the smaller boys, who had no part in filling the privy with snow, wanted to use it. He went out and came back promptly complaining impatiently to the teacher, because he was in a hurry. The teacher bundled up and went out for a look at the reported problem. The soft snow had turned hard, real hard. That boy's toilet was now filled to the shingles with one solid block of ice because of the severe drop in temperature over night. It could not be removed. You could have torn the siding and frame down and the solid cake of frozen snow would have still remained. Not a single country boy's warm butt melted the hoary frost from a hand whittled privy seat for quite a spell. In fact, not for the rest of the winter. The teacher was exasperated. The school board was mad. The boys were frightened to death. The teacher whipped them. Their fathers about incapacitated some of them in the old woodsheds with the leather belts. The whole community was mad at them. The girl's toilet had to do double duty under strictly timed regulations. To make matters worse, this was a year when there was no January thaw. What an inconvenience caused by some prankish boys with wet snow! They had planned to dig it out the next morning, only they couldn't. By then it was a serious situation. Now, it is a lead topic and good for a big laugh anytime two or more of those former pupils get together.

"Remember the day the boy's outhouse was frozen full of snow, and there was no inside plumbing? Boy! Did I get a beating!"

Christmas Exercises

Christmas at the country school circa 1900 was a main event for every family in the district whether they had children of their own taking part or not. It was called the Christmas Exercises or the Christmas Program.

Preparations began as soon as the gobblers were removed from the schoolhouse windows.

The main cog was the schoolteacher. She was hired by a three-man school board, who had the titles of Moderator, Treasurer and Director. She was paid $35 a month. For this amount she owed her very soul, not to the "Company Store," but to the community of that particular school district. Among other things, it was part of her job to put on the annual Christmas Exercises.

The dear teacher was expected to run the show. She was the director, mistress of ceremonies, prompter and the goat, if she did not put on a better exercise than the one last year. This was a critical undertaking for a new or very young teacher. It was her first baby.

There were many things to be done. The first move was to develop a program in which every last pupil would have a part. She assigned the parts and did not take no for an answer. The pupil was given a week to memorize his recitation, song, or lines in a play, before practice began at school as part of his language class.

These parts were learned so they could be repeated frontwards, backwards and while asleep; but when the great moment came with everybody in his world waiting in anticipation, nary a word could be remembered. One would stand there with one foot atop the other and fidget. Another would cry, or in reverse, break out in a silly grin. The teacher would come to the rescue — after she thought they had suffered enough — as prompter.

I vividly recall my first contribution to a one-room country school Christmas Program. It was a short four-line verse.

"Here I stand
All ragged and dirty,
When Santa comes to see me
I run like a turkey."

On the last line I was to run down the aisle to my mother. Anxious to start the run, I tripped over my own feet and fell flat on my face. There was no damage except to my pride and the fact that it seemed to set a pattern for my life.

Of equal importance were the tree and Santa Claus.

The big eighth grade boys already had a tree picked out and asked for in the nearby forest. It had to be tall enough to touch the ten-foot schoolhouse ceiling and strong enough to hold up a heavy burden for a few hours.

Santa had to be fat and jovial with a deep voice and a stranger to the children of the district. He was expected to arrive at the precise time and alight from his cutter with a bulky bag over his shoulder. Ho! Ho! Ho! He would pass out at least one present for each person in attendance. A small bag of hard candy, a popcorn ball or a handmade item.

The overworked teacher usually hit the jackpot as to presents.

One year at the school Christmas Exercises, some dad tied a pup to the tree as a present for his boy. This pup stole the show until a kitten, wearing a red ribbon, was also placed on the scene. The kitten escaped from the pup's vicinity by climbing to the top of the Christmas tree.

This was the best decorated tree we ever had. Pup on the bottom, decorated kitten on the top.

Standard tree decorations were strings of popcorn, cranberries, colored paper chains, and a big star on the topmost branch. Lighted candles were not allowed because of the fire hazard.

This was the only Christmas some families had, so it was important.

Of course, the major components were the program, the tree and a jolly good Santa Claus; but there were other things that could make a young schoolteacher middle-aged before her time.

One was the matter of lighting. In the 19th century coal-oil bracket lamps with mercury reflectors were used. Later, gasoline mantle lamps provided much better lighting but were forever needing pumping up or refueling. The lighting at the Christmas Exercises was always a source of anxiety.

Another was the forgetting of a necessary prop. For instance, "Elsie forgot to bring her angel wings," or "What happened to the prompting notebook?"

There had to be snow for sleighing to make it complete. The schoolyard would be parked full of beautiful horses hitched to various bobs and cutters. The horses would get cold and restless. Sometimes a horse would break loose and take off for the road and home, often upsetting a couple of other rigs in his getaway. This would disrupt the Exercises but not cancel them.

As soon as the last strains of Silent Night faded from the pump organ, you would hear the song leader asking the crowd to please pass the Knapsack Song Books to the front of the room.

Then, and not until then, did the most important event on the program surface — socializing.

People lived far apart then. This was the golden opportunity for greeting, showing off the new baby, exchanging ideas, sizing up the neighbor's hired girl, planning for the future and catching up on the latest gossip.

The fire in the old potbellied stove that was in the center of the "one-roomer" was dying down. Some of the lights had expended their fuel, and couples with sleeping children in arms gradually drifted out to their sleighs leaving the country school to the young for "courtin."

These were the ingredients that made for a grand and great Merry Christmas — except for one final development that was the opposite of "Peace on Earth, Goodwill Toward Men."

There was bad trouble in the woodshed; what a commotion! We boys got over being sleepy real fast and decided to investigate. Three determined young farmers were into a free-for-all with the winner to take all. Take what? Why, the young "schoolmarm" home. It did not make much sense to us boys as we watched the fighting through a crack in the woodshed door. The years have changed me. Now I understand.

REINCARNATED
Most of the one-room country schools have been demolished. Some have been restored in various communities as historical buildings. A few have been rebuilt and are being used as homes, such as the steading pictured here located in Clinton County, Michigan.

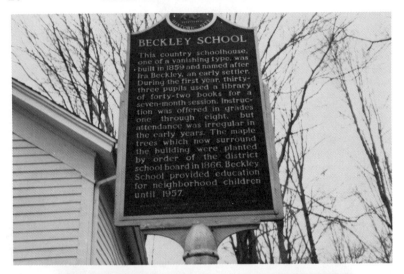

TWO COMMEMORATIVE MARKERS

The humorous memories of some one-room country schools exist only in the minds of our elderly citizens. These recollections will soon be lost forever. A few of these institutions of lower learning have been commemorated by various local projects. Here are two.

CHAPTER II

THE COLTS

BECAUSE I WAS reared during the horse and buggy era, young boys from the time they began to scamper and cavort about until they attained the age of puberty were commonly referred to as colts. Sometimes, extremely wild specimens were called mustangs and several other less complimentary names, like crazy alecks, wildcats and smart arses. They were expected to assume responsibility for some chores and a few other light tasks, like fetching cool water to the field hands, but most of their time was spent prancing about and kicking up their heels.

Should, perchance, some individual within the family take an aversion to their senseless activity, a patriarch would customarily speak out in their defense.

"Let the boys alone. There will be plenty of work left for them to do when they grow up."

Stone Picking

One of the few tasks allocated to lads was picking up stones. This was a perfect example of why early settlers had large families and always preferred that they be heavy with boys.

When new ground was being wrested from nature, men and teams of horses (or oxen) would snake out the deadheads and other loose rocks that were larger than a sap bucket. All other rocks were the responsibility of the boys.

These smaller rocks were called stones and were usually so thick on the ground that you could step from one to the other. Fields were small. Stones could be disposed of by pitching them on a pile in the middle of the lot or into the surrounding rail fence rows. Some of these same boys developed strong arms and became great ball players.

This job would take place in the heat of summer while the new lot was being fallowed for wheat. Each time it was harrowed with an A-tooth drag, more rocks would see the light of day. This required another stone picking session. The job was never ending. It would have been intolerable except for the fringe benefits.

One benefit would be having your best friend not over half a step away at all times. This was your personal dog. Your dog would clobber mice, meadowmoles, snakes, weasels, woodchucks and skunks. You were on a perpetual big game hunting expedition. It was a fantastical world of make-believe in which a deer mouse was called a ten-point buck, a groundhog a lion, etc.

Another plus was the finding of Indian relics in these small fields of virgin soil. They were never considered prized possessions, just swapping material. Sometimes they were used as conversation pieces in this way; boys contested each other over who could spin the best yarn about the travels or nefarious activities of the Chippewa Indian arrowhead or the Ottawa tomahawk which was currently wearing a hole in his pocket.

The greatest reward came at the close of day just before climbing in between his mother's cool clean sheets. It was the nightly bath. On a hot dusty job like throwing stones a lad wore two pieces of clothing, a straw hat and his britches. If the summer fallow was dry, so that each time he put his foot down a puff of dust came up his pant leg and joined the sweat which was running in the opposite direction, he would become coated with many layers of dirt. This classified him as a live mummy.

Somebody at the house would know about the condition of his body, minus straw hat and britches. To remedy the situation and keep those feather ticks clean, a tub of water would be drawn and set out on the back lawn to warm in the afternoon sun. Beside the tub would be soft soap and a towel. The bathing ritual began as soon as the sun completed its journey. The first one in used sparkling water. With each succeeding bather the water became roilier. Also, there would be less water and more sand in the bottom of the old wash tub.

It mattered little whether the lot he drew for his turn in the tub was first or last, it was the greatest of feelings. He went into deep sleep the minute he hit the bed and slid in between those clean sheets. Oh! For the life of a country boy.

Gnaw the Peg

A jackknife in his pocket was the badge that signified a boy had attained the rank of a colt. His first acquired talent was how to put an edge on the blade of his jackknife by using the grindstone. In connection with this, his first personal possession, besides the shirt on his back and the pants on his bottom, was this jackknife.

There were precautions that had to be taken. First, the knack of using the weapon had to be mastered to minimize the number of slashed fingers and punctured thighs. A statement from an elder on the matter of a colt cutting himself up would be like this: "Cut away, cut away, draw not the blade toward you."

There was a game of skill played with a jackknife called "mumblety-peg." Attached to this game as a penalty for the loser was "gnaw-the-peg."

It required from three to six players seated in a circle on a patch of sod, with knives in hand. Two of the blades were opened. The longest at 180° and the smaller at 90° to the handle. The rules were flexible. All players were required to flip their knife in the

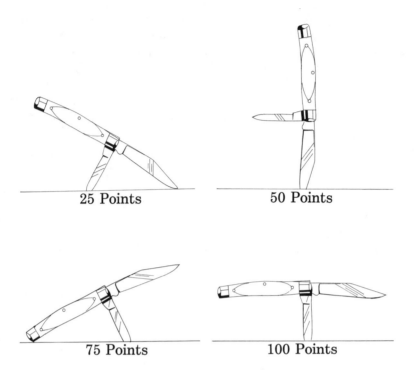

25 Points   50 Points

75 Points   100 Points

MUMBLETY-PEG SCORING

same style over their wrist or hand with the object of sticking it in the sod in one of the following positions, for points as designated.

Whoever made a thousand points first won the game. Whoever ended up with the smallest number of points was the loser and had to "gnaw-the-peg" or he could not play again. He always gnawed.

A peg of wood about three inches long was whittled out of something hardy. It was driven into the ground by the players, minus the loser, by hitting it with the back of their jackknives. The winner was allowed two whacks. The others, one each. At whatever depth in the ground it ended up at, after the best efforts of the other players, the loser was required to get down on his prayer bones and pull that peg out with his teeth. Sometimes, if the winner and the other players had been able to drive the peg down to ground level or below, the loser would have to root away the dirt with his nose (no hands allowed) and gnaw out the peg with his teeth until he could get a secure enough hold on it to pull it out. If the loser was unsuccessful in lifting the peg with his teeth or refused to do so, he was thrown out of the game and sometimes even excommunicated from the herd of colts.

The Knife

The second precaution, after learning how to handle a knife so as to keep from cutting one's self, was not to lose the jackknife. That was a cardinal sin. If sown, a knife was not usually replaced and one was never known to sprout forth and replace itself as a kernel of wheat or a tree. The loser simply did without until such time as he accumulated funds to buy a replacement. This might be a year or two. The first one was a gift for a birthday or Christmas, but if a second one was needed, there was no duplicate gift.

Consequently, a colt would know the location of his knife every moment of day or night. The usual parking place was in his side pants pocket where the weight of it or the feel of it against his leg became so natural that the first second it was not there, he was immediately aware of its absence and began searching.

There was yet another most important reason for keeping his jackknife on his person. Before the colt became aware that there was a biological difference in youngsters, everyone not carrying a jackknife was scratched off his list and considered to be a girl or the next worst thing.

Duck on the Rock

An average day could be divided into this sort of schedule. After downing a horse-size breakfast would come morning chore time, followed by a few odd jobs like pulling weeds, cleaning and restrawing hen's nests and the likes. As soon as the sun got high enough to raise beads of sweat on your forehead, it was down the tracks to the swimming hole. Hunger dictated automatically the time to hit out for provisions. With a full belly, "gnawing-the-peg" was exercise enough for an hour or so. Then before the finale of skinny dipping there would be a session of rough-and-tumble called Duck on the Rock. One colt would mount a boulder and challenge anyone or all of them, collectively to drag him off. Possession of the perch could change several times with scuffed skin and bruised knees as the only reward for having succeeded in holding off fellow colts for a few minutes.

Swimming Hole

When I was as an unbroken colt, we had a secluded swimming hole. Actually it was a brush-hidden corner of a local spring-fed gravel pit.

If one rode a bicycle the way of the dusty gravel road it was nigh onto four miles. By the steel rails of an "as the crow flies" railroad, it was only two and one-half miles. A colt heading for the swimming hole took the short way, especially seeing as how the rails were so smooth on his bare feet.

When hunger pangs interferred, which was often, we hit for the wild strawberries along the Grand Trunk Railroad right-of-way. Later in the summer the black raspberries were ready and waiting. For meat we would pin down young bullfrogs in the high grass near the water. The number caught depended on the need. We would tap them on the head until they felt no pain and while they were in this state of immobility, we would disconnect their legs from the body, roll the thin spotted green skin down to their toes and cut the toes and skin off with one swipe.

This edible part of the bullfrog would be impaled on a forked green willow branch and roasted over a small fire. When the muscles of the frog's legs stopped twitching, they were ready to eat.

We never accumulated a supply; were never wasteful. It was one set of frog's legs at a time. Some days it would take many trips into the grassy wetlands before our appetites would be appeased. It was fun, every minute of it, because it was hunting, cooking out-of-doors and eating. Grown men today attempt to copy the life style we enjoyed as colts. The only thing that differs is the cost of their toys versus the cost of ours. The intent and rewards are the same.

There are a multitude of fine eateries in the perimeter traveled by this emaciated old horse. They advertise and brag on the quality of their frog leg dinners at a fancy price. I have tried them in various highly recommended locations, but have always come away disappointed. They do not measure up to the quality of those we cooked beside the swimming hole when I was a colt.

Mention of that old swimming hole makes chills run up and down my spine for two reasons.

One was when we arrived at our swinging tree. It hung out over the blue water of our private hole. We would run the last quarter of a mile to see who could hit the water first. Oh McNally! It was so cold. It was spring fed and very deep, perhaps all of forty feet. The contrast in temperature between that of our hot little bodies and the icy water was paralyzing. I would say that we were not presumptuous in assuming, as we grew out of the colt stage, that it was sheer luck that one of us did not lose his life in that swimming hole. It was cold and deep, but so refreshing. It was not a water that you could dive into, touch bottom and bob back up. By opening your eyes as the momentum of your dive slowed and looking off into the depths, it was like a black hole into the space of the universe. The gravel was removed from this pit by a powerful pump with a sucker pipe mounted on a pontoon, rather than by a mechanical dredge; so no one living knew the depth. The previous mention of forty feet was an arbitrary figure.

The remaining reason that chills do play games with my spine when our antics around this swimming hole are recalled is because we nearly did lose one of the colts in that dark cold hole before we outgrew it.

The near casualty was a colt who never caught on to the knack of swimming. He was one of the younger ones, slight of build, wiry as an ironwood sapling, and gutsy. Most of his activities in the water were close to shore. An old-timer had told Doyle that if he would jump in over his head he would begin swimming by instinct. Doyle had told us he was going to try it someday when he felt real cocky and had plenty of frog legs in his belly. The old-timer had provided Doyle with lots of proof which he told to us. I remember a couple of his arguments. They were out in left field and rattled like stones in a tin can; such as — dogs swim real good by instinct — clumsy horses can swim a stream and pull a wagon too; who taught them? — nature took care of swimming lessons for pollywogs.

"Hell, Doyle, you are smarter than dumb animals. You can swim."

That particular day the colts had the end of a plank wedged under a boulder and over a log at right angles, to make a decent diving board.

Without a word of advance warning Doyle ran out on that plank, sprang it up once and yelled, "I'm going to swim."

He went into that dark deep cold hole feet first. We all stayed put, more in admiration than fear. We were not old enough to be frightened.

Doyle did not surface immediately. He did not come up after a watchful delay; period. We became alarmed. The oldest of the colts walked out on the plank and pointed off the end to a spot about where he had hit the water.

"I can see something down there that was never there before. It must be him."

Several of us walked the plank and took a quick look. We knew he had been down far too long. I was the closest in the little group to being a fish. I dove in the direction "of the something," with eyes open. It was Doyle! It was necessary to swim deeper than the dive carried me to grab a fistful of his black hair. He seemed to have passed completely out. There was no movement, no grabbing, no fighting back. I was soon out of air so a couple of the other fellows took over and I busted for the surface. They had him on shore in a jif. Doyle was blue as a whetstone and as limp as your mother's dish rag. We draped him over the boulder that was serving as ballast for the diving plank, pushed on him a couple of times, and a lot of water came out of him from somewhere. His eyes began to roll and he coughed. One of the Benear Twins had read something about artificial respiration in school. Benear worked him over.

Somehow between us, or because of the fact that Someone was watching over us, Doyle came around. I never did know if he was close to drowning, if he had suffered a concussion by jumping in the water the way he did, or if it was shock from the low water temperature.

Regardless of the cause, it had a sobering effect on that particular crop of colts.

After putting our clothes on, we made a secret pact that had to do with Doyle staying under the water too long. Doyle put it to us in this way. "If my folks ever hear of you fellows having to haul me out they will never let me come here again and perhaps you will get the axe, too."

His idea made sense. He was a leader. We decided to never mention the incident. From then on we were prancing colts no more.

The secret was never told. In three score of years it has not been made public knowledge, as far as I know, until this writing.

Doyle's mother, Myrtle, and father, Homer, have both passed away as well as the former colt. He enlisted in the Marines (he really was a tough gutsy guy) and was in the Death March on Bataan when the Japs had us by the throat. Fate decreed that he was to give his life for his country as a hero and not to lose it as a colt in the depths of the old swimming hole.

The elementary school in Lennon, Michigan, is named the Doyle Knight School in his honor.

A HERO'S MONUMENT

Comment

This episode does not exactly coincide with the mood of this book but the author feels good about putting it here as a personal tribute to a hero, Doyle Knight, with whom I was privileged to share some boyhood days.

CHAPTER III

SUGAR SHANTY

THERE HAVE BEEN many yarns spun and written about sugar shanties. Here are a couple of happenings that took place in that setting. One was a putrid day and the other a sweet, sweet night.

Our neighbor Roy had a beautiful rolling wood lot of hard maple trees that he tapped each spring. The wood lot was like a park. The few boys of the neighborhood were allowed free rein of this property and cherished it as if it were their own.

In the middle of these woods, erected on a well drained south slope, was a sugar house. It contained all the necessary equipment for making maple syrup from the sap that was collected from the trees. There was a large hearth, custom-built from stone picked up from the adjoining fields with the top row being of Middlesworth firebrick, so as to provide an even surface to set the sap pan on. The hearth would accommodate wood up to ten feet long. An elevated raw sap supply was anchored outback on the rise behind the shanty. It would gravity-feed into the evaporating pan on the hearth. The flow of sap could be regulated by a wooden spigot inside the shanty. There was a chimney for the smoke and an opening all the way around the cozy building at the eaves to let the steam from the boiling sap escape. There was a bunk for resting (you seldom found time to sleep) on each side of the leather-strap hung door. It opened on the south side directly

A WORKING SUGAR SHANTY

in front of the business-end of the hearth. Sometimes Roy would ram a dead sapling into the hearth twenty feet long, leave the shanty door open, and keep shoving it into the fire as it was consumed. This saved a lot of chopping. There were a few nails to hang your hat and coat on. Lordy! It would get hot in there even though it was built of rough-sawn hardwood boards. It had to have been nailed up when the lumber was green because the boards had warped as they cured and they were so hard you could not even carve your initials in them. You did not have to hunt for a knothole to see what was going on out in the woods. You could look out the cracks anywhere.

Precocious Sanitation Engineers

Roy, who liked kids, gave us boys the responsibility for keeping the place in order during the off-season. That was eleven months out of a year. The red squirrels would chew a set of leather hinges off the door every year and the "be-cussed" woodchucks would go back to work undermining the place as soon as our backsides went over the hill. When they had the dirt floor altered to their liking they seemed to move on to the next project and a den of skunks took possession or maybe ran out the woodchucks. We never knew exactly how the franchise changed hands.

A couple of us kids went back during summer vacation, which was a third of the year, with a couple of our mother's garden spades, with the idea of cleaning the shanty and leveling off the floor where the woodchucks had piled up mounds of dirt. We were about ten years old. When we opened the door the place did not look bad; but it sure smelled bad. Something had done a job at the edge of the hearth that looked like a pile of ground up crickets. Ken was the older and he knew about such things.

"Skunks eat crickets. I bet there is a skunk back in there," Ken said, as he pointed his spade into the dark hole under the evaporating pan which was greased and upside down on the arbor. We both got down on our knees with spades pointed inward. There was a rustle. We were gritty kids. No matter what was under the pan, it was taking its life in its own hands; only it was they.

The battle was decisive and disastrous for our side. Ken's new dog, Curly, was right in the line of fire with us. He was only a pup and he didn't know any better either.

It was a hot, muggy, late afternoon. The stench seemed to smother us. We both began to cry, cough, and spit, in that order. After we had each gone through the routine about three times, plus rolling in the grass like Curly, I saw Kenny button up his bottom lip. He was a real tough kid.

"Let's go over where Dad is," suggested Ken. He was across the road and south about twenty rods, hoeing corn and whistling.

We had come by him about an hour ago and all he had said was, "Don't you fellows get into any trouble with those big shovels." He knew what we were up to because we had planned it for a week.

Curly arrived at Charlie's corn row much ahead of us. He got a potent whiff of Curly, stopped hoeing, and began throwing clods of dirt at the dog to keep him away. Poor Curly took off for the barn with his yet undocked tail between his legs.

After the hostile reception Ken's dad had given Curly, we were a bit cautious in our approach. We could see from a distance that he was muttering something to himself. Of course, he had to have been watching our progress across the corn field from out of the corner of his eye, after being forewarned by Curly.

Suddenly, he dropped the hoe and held up both hands.

"Whoa! Don't come any closer. I've got corn to hoe. Go see your mother. Where're the shovels?"

We just pointed toward the woods. Of course, he knew exactly where they were. He put his head down and kept chopping corn. As we passed him on the windward side, we saw him shake his head and blow his nose real hard one time. We did not get any help there.

As we rounded the corner of the granary, Ken's mother, Jennie, was out with the broom lambasting Curly off the kitchen stoop. Lucky that we had Curly along or we might have got it the same way. Now we knew what to watch out for.

Ken blurted out between half sobs, "Curly was between and behind us when disaster struck. How could he smell so bad?" I

MEPHITIS MEPHITIS

Skunks are equipped to dig their own burrows, but seldom do. They are usurpers and would rather take possession of a woodchuck hole because they are roomier.

Their number one defense is a putrid spray. This spray will travel 20 feet against a strong wind and 4 miles with that same wind. When this sticky, greenish fluid strikes an intruder it causes choking, coughing, temporary blindness and even a possibility of a blackout. This debilitating material will dissipate with time and become only a lingering disagreeable odor.

didn't think he smelled too bad now, because I didn't notice it like at first when we lost the battle. My lips didn't even taste like they did at first.

We started toward the house. Jennie and Grandma Stein were both out on the stoop now. Curly stood about halfway between the barn and the house. His ears were down, his back was humped up, and he looked as if he did not have a friend left in the whole world. We were worse off, but did not know it.

"Kenneth! Kenneth! Do you hear me? If you ever let that pup of yours come to the house smelling like that again, we will have to do away with him." Grandma Stein stood right behind Ken's mother nodding her approval.

She continued to yell out toward us. "We almost gagged. He must have had a hold of a skunk's tail. Tie him up out in the orchard and come on to the house. I want to get you cleaned up and ready for that church meeting tonight. Stanley should go home, his mother will be wondering about him. You both look filthy."

When in trouble a country kid goes up into the haymow to figure things out. It was a place of solitude. A place to meditate. Up the ladder we went dragging Curly up with us. Why not? Curly had already saved our skins twice. He was a great pup and on his way to becoming a great dog. Right now, he really was the only friend we both had — for sure.

The first thing we did was smell each other all over like dogs do. Then we both smelled Curly. We came to the conclusion that none of us smelled very bad. I noticed that Ken's face, where the tears had not run, was thick with dark bluish-green specks and his clothes looked kind of a faded yellow all across the blue overall bib. I did not say "nuthin" about it even to him. We were tired and felt kind of sick and overcome by the whole thing. Shortly, the three of us curled up and went to sleep together in the haymow.

Ken's father woke us up in the morning by yelling from the top of the ladder at the opposite end of that mow of loose hay.

"Come and get it, you skunk hunters." We rubbed our eyes and bounced on the loose hay over to where he had left a pile of pancakes that were shedding melted butter down over their sides and about a gallon of warm milk. We figured that we were in for bad trouble for having slept in the haymow all night without permission. I did not even go home. My folks did not know where I was! We had done a thousand forbidden things. We would both get the razor strop, and good!

Charlie put us at ease real quick, for there he was already back down on the barn floor alternately standing and bending over laughing as hard as we had ever seen this big man carry on. Tears of laughter were streaming down over his jowls, as they had over ours the afternoon before from fear and the vile secretion.

"You fellows stay right where you are and keep Curly with you. We don't need any of "youse" down here. Grandma Stein will be out here in a bit. She is going to give all three of you a bath from head to foot with her homemade soft soap and vinegar. After she finishes with you guys, you hold Curly for her. Hang your dirty clothes in the tool shed. She is going to bring you clean ones as soon as Stan's dad brings his down."

"We don't stink anymore," we said. Charlie just held his arms up to the heavens and walked out of view. At least my folks knew where I was. That was a relief.

We shared the milk and pancakes with Curly. By noon, we both had our feet under our own mother's dinner table, and life for the sugar shanty janitors was back to normal.

Ken and I were amazed by the lack of punishment and the few remarks that were made about the commotion we had caused. Finally, when we could stand the suspense no longer, we asked Steven Hatch, my dad's hired man, what he had heard about us, if anything.

We were playing it safe by going through a third party. Steve was a blunt, rough talking guy, who would do most anything for us boys.

"Nobody had to say anything," he said. "We could smell ya a mile agin the wind. Ya still stink! I had to bury your mother's spade out in the garden, don't know if she can even use it agin. We don't want the thing around the barn. What in the world did you do, walk in on a den of skunks while they were having a p------g contest?"

The Sweet Night Shift

The spring that followed our losing the battle with the skunks turned out to be a fine one for the making of maple syrup. A spell of abnormally warm weather had blown into this mitten of Michigan on a southwest wind. Did it make the sap run! The supply tank was full and the buckets on the trees were running over before neighbor Roy realized it.

Roy had tapped the trees only a couple of days before so that this would be all choice first-run syrup. To keep the pails from running over, it was necessary to gather sap from the trees three times a day and maintain the evaporator at a rolling boil around the clock.

Our neighbor had sap literally running over the top of his boots. In addition, he had livestock chores to do and a responsive young wife to look after, so he asked Ken and young Perk if we would spell him in the sugar shanty one night. We jumped for joy at the invitation. There was no money involved; pay never entered our minds. The maple syrup was only fetching two dollars for an eleven pound gallon and you could buy a new pair of mittens for fifteen cents. Money was of no account. This opportunity to help a friend was of more consideration and besides he would help us out should we ever get in a jam.

Roy suggested that we go over to the chicken coop and help ourselves to a dozen eggs.

"You fellows might get hungry before morning," he said. "Don't let the fire go out or the pan boil dry."

It was a big all-night responsibility for a couple of kids. Our folks never worried about us. This was our way of life, and we loved every minute of it.

Getting back to the food, we filled our pockets in the chicken coop so we might have had two dozen eggs instead of one. Who cared? They were only worth ten cents a dozen and you had to trade them for groceries to get that.

Upon arriving at the sugar shanty to relieve Roy, we put all those eggs into the pan of boiling, rolling, frothing maple sap. Every time we felt a little hungry, we would take the skimmer down from its hook and fish out two or three apiece. They were real good. The sap added a sweet taste as egg shells are porous.

All that we had to drink throughout the night was cold sap from a bucket that hung on the nearest maple tree. So there we were — a pair of country kids with a big all-night job to do and getting sweeter by the hour.

Roy knew best. We should have taken his advice. One dozen eggs would have been enough. We polished off those eggs washed down with a generous supply of raw cold sap, and nothing else. No salt, pepper, cheese, crackers, bread, cookies; no "nuthin."

We both came down sick with the heaves in the middle of the night — real sick. Ken would go outside the shanty and throw up while young Perk was stoking the fire. Then we would switch. It got to be routine. We both became so sick that the fire nearly went out one time, but we had to stay with it. We could not let Roy down, even though we thought at least one of us would die right there in the woods outside Roy's sugar shanty before the night was over.

I remember asking Ken one time, "Have I turned inside out yet?"

"Nope," he replied, "I think you are going to make it. You just look like a puckery green apple. Green apples come around, if you don't touch them until they get ripe. I think I am the one who is going to die. When I look away, everything looks cloudy. Sometimes I feel like I am floating on a big white cloud. Perk, do you think I am on my way to heaven?"

"Ken, how could you be on your way to heaven after all the deviltry we have been into lately? How about the time we threw the dead snake in the vent of the preachers privy?" Of course, we didn't know his wife was inside and there was no reason for her to head for the manse with her drawers down showing her fat pink bottom and screaming bloody murder. The snake was stone dead. He couldn't hurt her. "We were lucky nobody saw us with that dead spotted adder before we found a place to put it. The fiery preacher would have burnt us at the stake."

"How about the time last week when we switched those rotten hen's eggs we found in the straw stack for some fresh ones in your mother's basket and took them to Pat Cook's Store, and traded them for licorice? Remember Ken, how we smeared the handle of the hired man Ed's favorite dung fork with fresh cow manure? We cannot die here now. We are not ready. We have to live because neither one of us is going to heaven."

This series of recollections shook Ken up and he decided that we would fight it through the night and not give up. Once in awhile Ken would bring up something about Sunday School.

"Perk," he probed me, "did that whale puke up Jonah because he puked in the whale's belly? I know just how Jonah felt. I couldn't stand any whale blubber either right now. You know Perk, it must be terrible to die if we are only half dead now."

By this time there was a ray of light in the eastern sky. This was a sure sign that help was on the way. Dawn was making a good wide crack, when we heard Roy's team coming with the "pun."

"Whoa, Nel" was one of the finest sounds we had ever heard in all our young lives. Roy opened the shanty door and started to shove more wood into the hearth when he turned and got a look at us.

"Say, what has happened to you fellows?" he asked. "You are green. Come over here in the light so I can get a good look at you. My land!" Roy exclaimed. "Look at this pile of egg shells! That's what the matter is. Climb inside the sap tank on the pun and lay down. Let me build up the fire a bit then we will skid you fellows on home to your mothers."

We laid real quiet on the bottom of the sweet smelling sap tank. We did not say a thing. It wasn't necessary. It had all been said for us.

The ride home was fuzzy. I did not remember much about it. Roy had it all figured out when he mentioned the pile of egg shells and the sweet, sweet sap.

I was fifty years old before I could look at a boiled egg without gagging and maple sap fresh off the tree still spins me out.

of quote and end of deer hunting for him and his cohorts for many a year.

$1000.00 Goldie

It was a day for duck hunting. Everything else was of secondary importance. It had been especially set aside as the day that the rich city cousins were coming out to shoot that duck and to try out their new $1000.00 Golden Retriever. It was an annual affair. Things looked good. The weather was even cooperating. A light blow was heading in from the northeast with low scudding clouds that were lending a hand with a cold drizzle. The ducks would be coming in on the lake fast and low.

As dawn was making a wee bit of a crack, the blinds were manned. Manned by three city cousins rigged out in the finest of shooting irons and clothing. A country lad in his barn boots and cow-hair covered mackinaw, plus the expensive well-trained Retriever called Goldie, completed the shooting party. They had no more than settled down in the heavy marsh grass when in came a flight.

Ca-whoom, ca-whoom and a duck cartwheeled into the water! Goldie, the new Retriever, was released and told to go fetch. That dog walked right out "thar," picked up the duck ever so gently, and walked right back to the blind. This was too much for the country lad. He took off on a dead run up the lane. He had seen a lot of dogs come and go, but never anything like this one.

A neighbor, Robinson, had two dogs that were quite unusual. The blonde dog was the front door dog. The black dog was the back door dog, but this Goldie dog was something else. No one at the farmhouse would believe the lad, as he tried to convince them that this new $1000.00 dog walked out upon the lake and brought a duck back to the blind the same way — by walking upon the water.

Only old Granddad would appease the country boy in the least. He agreed to walk back to the lake and see what in the world had disillusioned his grandson. He wasn't doing anything, no how, except rocking. Well, the country boy set Granddad up where he could see the whole show. It was a good day for shooting and in a middlin' amount of time a duck was brought down in the water. Out goes the Goldie dog, walking on the water right to the flopping duck, picks it up and walks back to the blind. Pow! Ca-whoom! Another flight comes in. Another beautiful retrieve follows. All this time, Granddad utters not one word of praise or amazement. At last, the country boy could wait no longer.

"Granddad, did you ever see anything like that? Isn't that a great dog? Did you ever in your life see a dog walk on the water? Tell me, what do you think?"

Finally, after rubbing his chin for a spell, he replied, "Son, that dog is no good. That dog can't swim."

The Brave Grandpa

This is a short bare bear story. Grandfather wanted to do something different to entertain the family. He planned a hike into some of the heavy forest of Neebish Island that is divided from Canada's St. Joseph Island by the narrowest channel of the St. Mary's River. Some of the area is very remote. Wildlife abounds. What a place to go tramping about, and so it was; the forest in all its solitude was overwhelming. Many signs of wildlife and their activities were observed.

Down by the foot of a draw, a good size spruce was suspended at about a 45 degree angle. The top was hung up in some other tree or else it would have gone completely over. The pine was also anchored by its root system. This system together with the forest moss, sod, and black dirt had suspended a couple tons of material and at the same time opened up a goodly sized cavern into mother earth.

This monarch of the forest was examined thoroughly by the family hiking party. There had been some game activity about the hole left by the heaving of the roots of this large tree. Some berry bushes near by had been trampled. Some limbs and sticks on the

I DARE YOU

A Black Bear in hibernation is not always asleep, just lethargic. This hibernating sow bear was nervous but displayed no hostility until disturbed. She was sheltering two small cubs with her body in the nest she had made for them. Photo by Frank Morgan

ground were broken as if something heavy had repeatedly walked over them.

Down on his knees for a closer look, Grandfather exclaimed, "There is a bear track right here in this soft dirt."

Without saying another word, the fearless sire of this family that had ventured into the wilderness, stepped back into the underbrush, picked up a stick about an inch in diameter, all of four foot long, and rotten to the core. He scraped the moss off his weapon and announced to all to watch out; for he was going down into that hole to see if it was a bear den — or not!

Grandfather disappeared on his hands and knees into the hole and under the upturned roots of this pine tree. Other members of the hiking party, including daughters and their children, backed off in amazement without speaking a word of objection to his bold action. Grandfather didn't keep them waiting for long. He returned on all fours with a triumphant smile on his face.

"There is no bear in there today, but there has been."

As he came out and stood upright at the mouth of the hole the youngest of the group asked, "Grandpa, what would you have done if there had been a bear back in that hole?"

This question by a mere youngling brought Grandfather back to reality. He turned stark white. He began to tremble like a leaf. All at once he looked twenty years older. He crumpled into the bushes. He had fainted away.

Bear Facts

There was a hunter who was exceptionally brave. He went out bear hunting with a bow and arrow. After a few hours he returned and everyone in camp crowded around seeking information.

"Did you have any luck?" they asked.

"Yep. I had excellent luck."

Hurry, tell us what happened."

"I didn't see a single one," was the answer.

Back in the hinterlands at a fork in the road of a previously

HOW IS THE FISHING?

unmarked trail, was a piece of pine plank cut with a jigsaw to resemble the shape of a Michigan black bear. It was nailed about eye high on a tree.

Engraved into this wooden bear were four letters, "L E F T." Not expecting a mind boggler in the backwoods it took a moment to decipher it. I hit up the left fork and arrived at my destination without difficulty.

Smelt Camaraderie

Everyone who resides within a convenient driving distance of the Great Lakes should go on a smelt safari, at least once. It is enjoyable and contagious. If you go once, the odds are that you will continue.

Because of an experience that is reiterated here, it is my personal observation that only one-half of the population goes a-dipping smelt. I believe that is a fair statement. The half who remain at home, snug, dry and clean, should have a firsthand account of what a smelt dipping excursion is all about.

Most people can only go on weekends. Regardless of your occupation, by Friday you have given over one hundred percent of yourself to someone else. You are tired out physically and wrung out emotionally, but the smelt could be running (an occurrence which only happens occasionally on weekends in early spring), so tired or not, off you go.

There was the appointment to take your step-mother to the doctor, you should get a couple of loads of gravel for the driveway, the snow shovels should be put away for the season, and the same with the fish spears, before they begin to rust. There are a thousand other things to do. Nix! Let's go get the smelt.

Here are some of the fortifications you will need to place you in the category of a Super Dipper.

Begin with the proper attitude. Smelt do not run when it is convenient for you to get them. They seem to intentionally skip those convenient days. They also prefer the wee hours of the morning. This is not all bad. There are a lot of diversions to be had while you are waiting for those silver flashes.

It is important that you move into this excursion with an open mind, perhaps with the attitude of a professional gambler. He knows there are always odds to be considered.

Your physical condition should improve as the miles are put behind. Skip the watering holes. Think smelt. It is the best of therapy. You will feel stimulated and aroused without altering your body chemistry. Later, maybe.

Let us move from the psychological to the tangible. Each person in your party should have his own long-handled smelt-dipping net. It is as important as having your own fishing pole; also your own pair of waders that come up as high as under your chin with non-skid cleats on the bottom side. None of those old smoothies should be tolerated as subsequent events will prove. Fetch along a lantern or some other dependable source of light, because you will be stumbling about in unfamiliar surroundings. A jackknife, matches in a waterproof container, and a bedroll or some other provision for a "lay me down" are musts. Oh! I almost forgot the most important item. Bring a food chest or some similar container to hold the smelt.

Don't forget to bring along your best go-getter attitude which I mentioned in the beginning. If you have this, everything else will fall into place — maybe.

Smelt are unpredictable. They either do or they don't. Some say a warm spring shower helps. I like a soft south wind. It seems to put the jacks into a courting mood. Sometimes all signs fail and it is not unusual to arrive at the precise spot at the right time, like 2:17 a.m., exhausted, and they do not show — and yet — did you see that silver reflection in the beam of the moon? Could that have been the end of the run or was that the beginning? Search me!

You stand patiently in an ice cold stream, right up to your you know what, for what seems like hours. Once in awhile you test the waters with the net just to keep your blood from solidifying. Someone downstream yells, "I got one!" In due course, you go partially numb.

You even forget to spit, and swallow the whole of that triple pinch that was inside your lower lip. While bending over trying to cough it up, in almost mid-stream, you lose your foothold on that slippery moss covered rock and pitch sideways into the water with a great splash.

They drag you out before the icy current drags you under, to the near shore, up a steep grassy bank and over to a seat on a log beside a roaring deadwood fire. You are wet, chilled and somewhat frightened. You think, "I should have stayed home and rotated the slabs of salt pork." Your teeth chatter, you shake and almost roll. But you never realized that you had so many friends.

Someone took charge. All others were doers. Orders flew from out of this fellow's mouth as if he had done the same thing many times before. Maybe he was an ex-drill sergeant in World War II.

"Build up the fire!"

"Get off his jacket."

"Pull off those waterlogged waders. They are keeping the water on the inside. Get it on the outside."

"Go over in the bushes, get some branches to hang his clothes on."

"Take off all his clothes, except his underwear."

"You women wring him out. No! His clothes, and hang them on these branches up near the fire. Smoke won't hurt them."

"Who has a good bracer? Give him a healthy snort."

"Now, these orders are for you. Start moving around, but do not leave the fire until you are dry. Congratulations, you are now a full-fledged Super Dipper. You will never know you were so waterlogged within a couple of hours."

A slap on the back was so zestful that it stung through your wet underwear.

"I'm Walt from Waterford. Where are you from?"

Before this newly initiated fraternity brother of the Super Dippers could answer, "Duffield," a mighty shout arose from a hundred voices all up and down the bursting young river.

"They're in! They're beauties!"

Immediately, the fireside became naked. It was completely decamped except for one person. You know who that was and in his soggy underwear.

To this day, I have not seen Waterford Walt. He broke ranks with the rest. To you Walt, I am forever grateful, wherever you are. Our meeting was humorous, it could have been tragic, yet it was a practical example of camaraderie among outdoor-loving people.

The Great Northern

There are fish stories and there are fish stories. This is one of utter frustration and of a mature gentleman whose word was so highly regarded that he was popularly labeled the mayor of his community. His wife, a most devout person, was the only witness. You have to believe.

He hooked into something really big right off the end of his boat dock with a light spinning reel using a frozen smelt for bait. It was twenty minutes of reeling and running before he caught the first glimpse of a Great Northern. The odds were with this trophy, from the beginning. The tackle was light, the monster was not hooked well and the only landing net available was twice too small. The twenty-five or thirty pound Northern Pike tired. Mayor Francis was able to get the fish's head in the net. He lifted the net, but there was more weight outside the net than on the

HAPPY YOUNG FISHERMAN
And proof that there are young sports too.

inside, so the fish flopped back into his natural habitat. He took
off on a run of fifty yards toward the great deep beyond before
Francis Williamson was able to convince him otherwise.

The route back toward the inadequate landing net was devious
and tiresome for both the fish and fisherman. The second attempt
was exactly as the first, except as the fish counter-balanced his
way out of the net, the hook tore from his mouth. The fish was all
in but his fins. He lay still in the water unattached to anything.
He rolled over on his side exposing a tremendous white belly.
Francis thought, "This is my monster from the deep." This was
the largest fish he had ever seen. It surely was a specimen he
would have mounted as a trophy for all those who entered his
home to admire. The fish was his now, for the picking up out of
the water. The mayor continued to have a series of wonderful
thoughts as he jumped right into the water to retrieve his prize.
His intrusion did not revive the fish. He continued to lay there
immobilized. Slowly but surely, Francis prepared to insert his
strong hands into the gills of this, his trophy catch. He was only a
couple of inches away and all set for a quick final grab, when he

was blinded by a great splash of water as the large Northern disappeared into his favorite haunts about Moon Island.

Francis has said very little about the incident to this day, but resumes the shaking of his head from side to side when anyone mentions fish or fishing. His wife is most understanding and hopes the shock of this loss, that has somewhat incapacitated the Mayor of Rocky Point, will pass in time.

A Trophy Muskie

Fishing has been almost a way of life for me; it is a wonder that I became a cattleman rather than a commercial fisherman. Perhaps that would have spoiled it all. As it is, fishing has been kept recreational.

In a recreational fishing career, there are goals and/or accomplishments one aspires to that correspond to those goals sought in a professional career. One of these ambitions has been to catch a trophy fish.

Several times, while trolling, I have hooked prospects. They all became unwilling cooperators because of inadequate equipment or bad judgment on my part. Thus a successful landing of a trophy fish never came to pass, but sooner or later, "every dog has his day." That day arrived.

He was raising havoc in Gogomain Bay not far from the remains of a great white ash tree that had ridden out of the forest on the ice of the spring breakup. It was Decoration Day.

Twenty fishing boats were in the immediate waters trolling for the walleye. In a sultry mid-morning sun, round and round, back and forth, they moved slowly through ideal ripples. Nite crawler harness was the lure. Patience was the attitude. Few landing nets had been wetted. Seeing as how the wind was in the south, this was most unusual and contrary to the following fishermen's homily:

When the wind is in the north
All fish go forth.
When the wind is in the east
Fish bite the least.
When the wind is in the south
It will blow the hook in their mouth.
When the wind is in the west
Fish bite the best.

So — everything was as right as it could be to insure excellent fishing — but they were not hitting.

I had noticed some unusual activity in the first quadrant of that bay. Small game fish and minnows of smelt size were breaking water and taking to the air. Their motive for this behavior could have been fun or fear. I played a hunch and bet on the fear. Was there a connection between the antics of the small fry and the temporary absence of the walleye? Had some behemoth of the deep moved in and taken over the territory as Lord and Master?

Perk went for the tackle box and searched out a certain lure that twice before had antagonized a great fish for other people. I attached this lure to the leader of the 30 pound test line on my great pole.

A trolling pass was directed toward the edge of the flying small fry activity that was now near the remains of the white ash.

Immediately, a shocking shudder shook the great rod, wrenched Perk's right arm at the shoulder and caused that reel to sing out like a saw in heavy timber as it gave up line. The Lord and Master of the Gogomain was hooked and he took off for the shelter of deep water. His exact course was well marked by the pattern of frightened small fish along his line of retreat. What a strike!!

The first mate put the boat in neutral and grasped the landing net. The deck was cleared for action even though the landing of this fish (if ever) was many minutes away. Trolling by adjacent boats ceased and all eyes were focused on this, the main event. It was to be a test of the strength of the equipment and skill of Perk up against the right to survive by the ruthless raider of this inland sea. However, neither of these factors were in consideration at the conclusion of the struggle. Would you believe it? The balance scale was tipped in favor of this fisherman by the first mate.

The battle was unique in this respect. The boat was reeled to the fish. Usually, the fish is reeled up to the boat. As pressure was maintained on the line, the hooked took to performing a series of circling tactics in diameters of about 10 feet.

Oh, he was an old hand at twisting lines. Those swivels must have warmed up.

His antics caused the water to literally boil to the surface as small fish continued to jump for their lives on the perimeter of his circle. These erupting boils, in which the ruthless raider never broke water, were closer and closer to our boat. The velocity never slackened. The fish did not tire. He never let up trying to throw the hook or twist off that 30 pound line.

A tremendous white belly flashed by on its dash toward security underneath the boat, but the first mate was alert. She had the landing net deep. It was in the right place at the right time. His huge head was in the mesh, but that was about all that could get in.

By now several minutes had elapsed. The show, which was being witnessed by the occupants of a circle of boats, could still go either way. The pole was useless at this point in the struggle and was dropped in the boat.

Perk's straw sombrero went into the drink and I went to the assistance of the first mate.

The fish was now identifiable. He was a Great Lakes Muskellunge of large girth and substance. His size would fill the net twice. He was never still a moment and acted like a bolt of lightning as we contained him temporarily betwixt the net and boat. There was no way to anticipate his next maneuver. So, we took the initiative.

Only a miracle would bring this muskie aboard.

And, believe it or not, a miracle happened.

Two loose hooks on the lure that were not in the muskie's mouth snagged in the net. He was what you call hog-tied to the net. There was no time for discussion. We heaved in unison. Halfway up the gunwale, the hoop attached to the handle of the landing net snapped. The two hooks entangled in the net broke away from the one embedded in his jaw — but the momentum of our combined lifting effort was just enough to roll the monster over the edge of the boat and into our control.

The heroine is the first mate because without her it would be just another fish story. The muskie is now a trophy.

I understand that the walleyes are back in Gogomain.

Spittoon Seekers

An addicted fisherman by the name of Willie B. brags that he has never been skunked on a fishing trip. When I asked him how in the world he could account for that phenomenon, I knew by the twinkle of his eye that I was asking for "the business."

"I seldom go fishing with the wind in the north but when I do go, I always go prepared to bring back fish," he said.

I thought to myself, that does not sound like he is giving me "the business." Why not stick around and listen to what the windbag has to say. So I did, but I was surprised that it was so brief. Willie B. had the reputation of possessing a healthy set of bellows which he could use when in a story-telling mood.

"How do you do it, Willie?" I asked.

"There is one way and only one way to get fish when they are not in a biting mood."

"First, select some good reliable person as a fishing companion. You will need him not so much as a companion, but as a witness. Nobody will believe you. Get all your equipment together; poles, tackle box, bait, landing net, extra line, sinkers, hooks, etc. Oh yes, don't forget to take along some good chewing tobacco. A small aluminum boat is best; so when you come back to shore with the fish you can flop it over and wash it out."

"Wash it out?"

"Sure, you will have more fish than you can get on your stringers. They will be in the bottom of the boat, too."

"Trolling motor?" I asked.

"Naw, you will not need a motor except to get to a place where you know there are fish. You will be kind of doing what is called still fishing. You could call it spot fishing. Throw in a set of oars or at least a long canoe paddle.

"The only thing that is not sure-fire about spot fishing is this.

You must go where there are fish. You have to go to them. If the location you decide on has no fish, you sure as hell are not going to get any inside your boat.

"Use your best judgment and drop the anchor so your boat will not drift. Don't touch the poles or tackle boxes. Get out your chewing tobacco and jackknife. Cut off small hunks from the plug about the size of a medium shot sinker and toss out a half dozen or so of these small pieces into the water about the boat.

"Get out an oar or paddle from under the seat. Watch closely. Sit up straight and stay alert. You have already noticed that the chunks of tobacco you tossed out have disappeared. The fish have grabbed them.

"When they come back up to spit, you hit them over the head with the oar. This is a sure way to get fish."

Monkey Making Pats

Have you ever been completely frustrated? Well, I have. I do not believe man evolved from a monkey but it can work in reverse — man can be made to look and to feel like a monkey in the flick of an eyelash.

The monkeyshines I refer to were precipitated by Bonasa umbellus, the partridge or ruffed grouse. It was a one-on-one confrontation. They made a monkey out of me by enticing me into their environment. Their environment is off — yes, far off — the beaten path. In fact, where they flourish there is no path.

I had just arrived on the scene at the dead end of a little-used gravel road. Had I continued further, I would have had to wrestle down a 12 foot aspen that stood defiantly in the middle of the tracks. Disembarking, I broke out the trusty fowling piece and took off gingerly on foot up an old logging trail.

I became thirsty. Somewhere in the distance, I picked up the sound of gurgling water. It was a welcome sound for this man soon to become a monkey. I headed in that general direction, ever mindful of my compass. That was insurance that I would return once again to the rat race.

SUCCESSFUL PAT HUNTER
He was lucky to bag a brace.

I walked down to a drinkable stream. It was sweet, soft water, definitely not polluted by minerals or chemicals. As I went to my hands and knees for the second draught, I was suddenly startled by an explosive slap on the water downstream.

By the time I responded, the only thing visible was an ever expanding ring on the calm water above a haphazardly built dam. It was a beaver dam. After a cautious period of time, a head surfaced nearer the crude dam. It was the landlord coming up for a look-see. He slapped the water again; I took the hint and moved out of his domain.

I moved carefully upstream and was soon encompassed by cedars. It was here I found the quarry and it was here that I was made into a monkey. With all the equipment and know-how accumulated down through the years as an outdoorsman, I was no match for the "pats."

All was quiet in the great forest. I continued to stalk my game by gliding around the outstretched guardian lower limbs of cedar, spruce, balsam and aspen. An eerie silence prevailed.

Suddenly, the quiet was rent asunder by a tremendous concussion of sound and motion. It was a single "pat" taking off from underfoot. My "shootin' iron" became entangled in some branches and I never brought it into firing position before the bird was out of sight.

Shortly, another one took off into a darting, diving flight, directly behind me. There was no chance to get off a shot because in twisting about, my feet became fouled up in the undergrowth and I fell down.

Feeling somewhat monkeyed, I moved on.

I flushed out six more but was successful in drawing a bead on only one. Instead of twisting and turning in low flight, this one took off unexpectedly almost straight up and over a 60 foot aspen. I was surprised as he executed a perfect screen pass pattern as he dropped over the top and out of sight.

In disgust, I pulled a mean trigger and blasted off into the great blue yonder. In a moment, the spent shot returned and sprinkled the leaves around me. Those "pats" had made a complete monkey out of me.

I ejected the remaining shells from my twice-barrel 12 gauge and began a three mile trudge back to civilization.

Arriving at the transportation, I cased the twice barrel and sat there a moment in a mood of restful reflection.

Darn fool! What would I have done "ifin" a "bar" had sniffed me out with no ammo in the gun? I was in heavy bear country. I began to shudder and shake and then it came to me. I was safe. Bear do not eat monkey.

As a Consultant

Animals are more intelligent than people in some respects. They imitate our life-style and do it often without having us become aware of it. Let me focus your thinking on an exemplification.

People who excel in their chosen field are seldom mustered out of a job brusquely. The process is smoothed over for both the employee and the employer by retaining the retiree on an intermittent basis as an emeritus, a part-timer or even as a consultant, subject to call.

This sketch has to do with a very domesticated feline. The resemblance I wish to emphasize is the result of his gradual development and his response to nature's call as he matured. The "he" being referred to is a much loved problem tomcat named David. David grew up beautifully from a playful, frolicsome tiger kitten. He was well marked with a white bib and white sox on his front legs. He had the silkiest slickest coat that ever crawled through the cat hole in a milkhouse door. He had large strong legs with oversize paws. He was extremely smart and alert, but he had a problem.

As the sun went down cloudy or clear, cold or warm, he would get out the door somehow and take off every night into the great beyond. Various tactics were tried to prevent his escape. Just when it was figured that he was cooped up for the night, some neighbor kid, a friend or salesman would open the door, and whoosh! Away he would go like a streak.

In the morning, early in the morning mind you, he would be at the same door scratching, begging and howling to get back in. Begrudgingly, out of sheer pity, the door would be cracked a wee bit. Then one could cast his sleepy eyes out upon the usual carnage. There he would be looking up and pleading for entry. What a mess to behold. Last night he was handsome. "Dave, look at you now." His coat would be matted and dirty, perhaps a drop of blood dripping from an ear. He would be gaunt and wobbly, his eyes would be glazed, but there would be a smile on his face. Pity would take control once again and he would be granted entry. His master tired of this routine, but still liked him and never entertained a thought of throwing him out permanently.

Eventually, there was absolute proof of his clandestine activities throughout the adjoining countryside. The womenfolk took particular aversion to these results, because their pet cats were fast becoming only one in a crowd. Their individuality had been severely diluted. One remarked that it was as embarrassing as buying a new gown for a local bash and observing upon arrival that most of the women were wearing the same dress. The entire area was becoming populated by cats that were marked the same as the sensuous David. Most were streaked tigers with a white bib and boots.

A family conference was held to discuss this plague that had descended upon the neighborhood. The veterinarian was contacted. He promised that after a fifteen dollar operation and a minimum of pain, David would be content to lay around the house and once again become a wonderful companion that affections could be lavished on.

The surgery was arranged, fifteen dollars was invested, but the result was not as promised. He soon returned to his same old routine of sliding out of sight at nightfall. When he returned each morning he did not appear to be in as bad a condition as formerly, but you could tell that he had done a lot of traveling. There would be sort of a professional look on his face. A complaint was made to the vet. He offered no alibi or comment on the quality of his work but made a simple suggestion.

"Why don't you follow this David cat in his nocturnal wanderings from a distance and try to observe what his hang-up is."

The vet's suggestion was followed. It wasn't easy, but the riddle was solved. David was only acting as a consultant.

DAVID
THE CONSULTANT

CHAPTER VII

RUNAWAYS

BECAUSE THE AREA encompassing the Great Lakes is so diversified, runaways assume a multitude of patterns. They have to do with the out of control mobility of animals, people and things.

Emphasis has always been placed on the tragic side of the news concerning runaways. Loss of life and property have snatched the headlines and dominated conversation, while the humorous incidents that make us smile have gone unrecorded.

The topic here will primarily pertain to hand-me-down accounts of the vices of horses and machines. Any other type of locomotion rated in horsepower is considered eligible for inclusion. This will justify a couple of transgressions.

Drayman's Wife Joins Circus?

Human runaways are purposely deleted so I will be careful not to mention them except to say, in passing, that no one ever forgot Sayde, the small-town drayman's wife, who tired of a ho-hum hum-drum existence. She came up missing the night a small circus pulled stakes after a one night stand. Some wags about town came up with the story that she had run away with the barker in that small circus. Others qualified the vamoose by saying that he would have had to hypnotize her to get her out of this town. Even though she and husband Floyd used to fight like cats and dogs and they had no family, she loved the hometown. Maybe?

As time rolled by, and with the passing away of Floyd the drayman, people always referred to Sayde as the local lady who ran away with the man in the circus. True or false, this could be classified as a runaway of convenience, or she did not love the town as much as the wags had calculated.

Wild Boat

Runaways have been known to originate within the waters of small inland lakes. This incident almost breaks the imaginary time barrier for my writing. It has to do with an early powerboat being operated by a pair of young women. I will not disclose the brand of the lapstrake hull but it was clinker built. The engine (now called motor) had most of its working parts exposed to the elements and was started by wrapping a pull rope around the flywheel.

The girls were properly attired for a muggy Sunday afternoon on the water. Soon several boats containing eligible young men were in pursuit. Engines roared and wakes ridged the small body of water to the extent that a few anglers, wetting lines, shook their fists at both the pursued and the pursuers. Back and forth they went, much to the entertainment of people at the cottages that lined the shore, until a roar from the boat containing the girls took on deafening proportions.

Immediately, the pursuers were left far arrears. People on shore gasped. The girls were working frantically over the controls. Seconds ticked off. It was obvious that at their speed the ship would be unable to navigate an abrupt turn that was only a few hundred yards off their port bow. Their engine had gone wild; something mechanical had happened, perhaps to the governor, so that the speed of the engine could not be throttled. It was a runaway!

In the face of this emergency the girls made the correct decision. They aimed that beautiful yellow clinker like a gun, straight into an unoccupied sandy beach and jumped overboard. The damage to the beach was minimal, but to the ship it was catastrophic. Oh, brother! Scratch one clinker.

For the young men in pursuit, it was good fortune. Naturally, they were the first on the scene and boated the beauties.

Logging Engine Gets Soused Too

On a tributary of the AuSable River called Honeywell Creek, a few miles northwest of Mio, Michigan, the forests were dense and the trees were great. Once it was thought that the sawmills in Mio would hum forever because the log booms that floated downstream were endless. The lumber barons knew better, but kept it to themselves. This held the lumberjacks in ecstasy.

Soon the timber was harvested back from the river for a distance of several miles. Narrow gauge railroads were constructed to bring the logs to the rollway as shown in the illustration. Most of the rail lines were temporary and only a few have been retained or restored. The one element they had in common was that they carried logs from the depth of the forest to the nearest waterway, where they could be floated downstream to a sawmill. It was natural that the narrow gauge came down from the highlands to the river valley and made a ninety degree turn. This placed the little engine, and its four to ten flatcars loaded with logs, in a position on the riverbank parallel to the flow of water. By releasing the chain binders the logs would usually spill into the water by themselves, being as how the riverbank track was always built on an incline.

After a couple of short blasts on the whistle it was no sweat for the engine to be reversed. They would ease around the curve and draw smoke, ash, and red hot embers through the stack from the

LOGGING ENGINE
Hauling logs to river for floating to the mill.

wood-stoked firebox as the engineer opened the throttle and backed up the hill and out of view.

It was payday. The last train of logs was on the cars. Everyone was tense. No drinking or women were allowed in camp. It had been thirty days.

The Porter Number 8 engine was throbbing on the rails under a full head of steam.

"Boss, she's got to go. That safety valve is ready to pop." On top of that, the firebox door was jammed full and red hot.

"All aboard."

Most of the loading crew piled on anywhere they could ride. Usually only two men accompanied the engineer. Why not go? It was the last load out this month.

Jack Flap was the engineer's name but it was hard to say, especially if you stuttered.

The lumberjacks reversed the words in his name about the same way as he reversed the little Number 8 narrow-gauge engine. It came out "Flap Jack" the same as the camp name for the giant buttermilk pancakes they put away by the stack before the break of dawn each morning.

The engine had about seven miles to travel to Honeywell Creek. The riders started yelling above the din of clattering wheels and hissing steam.

"More speed, Flap Jack — more, Flap Jack!" Against his best judgement, he opened the throttle a few extra notches. It was downgrade three quarters of the way. Jack Flap said to himself, "I will give those bearded bastards and their half-breed helpers the ride of their lives right down to the river curve, and set the brake and slide into the rollway."

His idea became a curve-swaying hair-raising experience and his freeloaders got the ride of their lives. He had them begging, for he could hear them pleading above the rushing air and engine noise.

"Hold her Flap Jack! Shut her down Flap Jack!"

What they didn't know was that engineer Jack Flap had been trying to apply the emergency brake on the Number 8 for the last eighty rods and it would not budge. He was a mighty man. He clutched the lever with both hands and braced his feet against the edge of the open firebox. It still did not move, but he snapped the handle right off at the ratchet.

He turned his back on the boiler and yelled out to the riders on the logs, "Jump! Jump for your lives! It's a runaway!"

They did. Jack Flap stayed with his little engine. He knew that it could never make the curve on the riverbank with the weight of the green logs pushing from behind.

Right you are, the logging train jumped the track at the curve and went straight on and into that branch of the Au Sable shoving the engine up against the opposite bank. Most of the logs broke their chains and went down the river as was the original plan. Engineer Flap waited and timed his jump so as to hit the water on the side opposite the tumbling bone-crushing logs. No one was injured. However, there were plenty of briar scratches, torn clothes and bent pride.

Jack Flap lost his job and was blackballed from ever again running an engine in the timber, because he was found guilty of highballing.

It was only partly his fault. He should have held his usual steady speed and not let the riders egg him on. After they had rebuilt the curve in the track and hauled the mess out of the river, a bolt of wood six inches in diameter was found wedged in between the brake control rod and the underside of the boiler. Because of this bolt the brake lever that engineer Flap wrenched off could not be moved. It was intentionally placed there by some disgruntled employee or picked up from the track and thrown there by the drive wheels.

It was always remembered as the payday that the Porter Number 8 ran off and got soused too.

Long Lake Horse Car

In the modern vernacular, this next runaway would be labeled a crossbreed. It was caused by a most unusual train of circumstances that took place both on land and sea and caused a dependable horse to spook.

The lake near Mt. Pleasant Post Office was a body of water nearly five miles long with a series of bays, coves and islands located in southern Genesee County, Michigan. It became the foremost resort area in the palm of the mitten and this large body of water was quite naturally called Long Lake. On its shore in 1857 was organized the Genesee County Pioneer Association. One of its Pioneer Picnics lasted a week and was attended by ten thousand people, even though the population of the entire state was scarcely twenty times that number.

In 1933 the name was changed to Lake Fenton because a Dr.

"CITY OF FLINT"
Under way with a good head of steam.

Mark S. Knapp of Fenton drew attention to the fact that Michigan had 106 Long Lakes. The runaway that was revealed to me took place at the time this lake was one of the hundred and six.

T.B. Case built a crude four-mast sailing vessel in 1856 to transport people to the island where the Pioneer Picnic was held the first couple of years. Many other small excursion boats, in turn, plied the lake. Afterward a steam excursion boat named "City of Fenton" was put in service by Eddy and Foster. They then decided to disagree for some unknown reason and severed their business relationship. Captain David Foster was soon plying the same waters with his own steamer, "City of Flint." They became fierce rivals for the lake business. They were always racing to the narrows to see who could arrive at the opposite dock first to take on board the people who were waiting there to become passengers. Meanwhile, people at the other end of the lake had a long wait for transportation, as long as two or three hours. The two captains and ship owners were bitter antagonists and it was about five years before the public could get them to alternate their

CAPTAIN FOSTER AT THE WHEEL
He was a robust competitor.

"CITY OF FENTON" and "MACCABEE"
Tied up outside the double-decked "Maccabee" at Bay Port on Long Lake

schedules so as to render more convenient service. However, the competition did not cease with that agreement; it was in reality only the beginning.

Finally, the resort and excursion business rivalry became so intense that Captain G.M. Eddy built a narrow-gauge track from the vicinity of the Fenton Hotel (still in business) to Bennett's Landing on the south extremity of the lake. It was a distance of about three miles. It went into service in the spring of 1891. This construction proved to be a profitable move.

Captain G. Marion Eddy had purchased his equipment from a defunct narrow-gauge rail line near Muskegon. It consisted of a few miles of steel rails and some horse-cars. They were transported to Fenton by flatcar on the Detroit and Milwaukee Railroad (Grand Trunk). A son, Charles S. Eddy, ran a livery stable in Fenton. He took care of the horses for the Fenton and Long Lake Line.

All inclusive excursion tickets were sold in Detroit (and elsewhere) for a pleasant morning train ride to Fenton Station. Captain Eddy's horse-car met the train and took them direct to his dock and to his ship, "City of Fenton." They were welcomed aboard for a leisurely cruise to Johnson's Landing at the north end of Long Lake after stops enroute at Cussewaga Beach and Bay Port. Picnic baskets were usually opened across the road from the north shore, in McCann's Grove. Swimming paraphernalia, and that is exactly the way you would define it today, was also utilized as the return of the steamboat was awaited. A convenient schedule of lake crossings was arranged so passengers could meet the late afternoon train on its return to Detroit and other stations. It all added up to a fine outing which was popular and well patronized.

Consequently, Captain David Foster and his ship "City of Flint" were suffering for business. Something had to be done; so he did it. Captain Foster caused a runaway, so thought Captain Eddy.

A horse-car full of well-dressed and well-heeled Detroit young people had just been unloaded with tickets in hand to board his competitor's ship, "City of Fenton." Captain Foster had heard said that there was yet another load waiting at the railroad station for transportation to the lake.

HORSE-CAR
Calculated by Captain Foster to be unfair competition.

A beautiful large gelding was used for power on this day. The car carried twenty to twenty-five passengers and rolled on the steel rails with a minimum of effort. Manual braking had to be done on the grades to keep the car from rolling up on the power supply. In other places on the route, where it was upgrade, the big gelding had to do some lugging. He pulled the horse-car from a path between the rails with a singletree attached to the tugs of his ornate harness. Many of the big city people liked the horse-car ride through the countryside as well as they did the steamboat ride on the lake.

The outing was a series of enjoyable rides from train to horse-car to steamboat and return. There was always a bustle as transfers were made from one conveyance to the other. So it was, when passengers got off the horse-car to embark on the boat this summer day.

For a moment the horse and attached empty car were left unattended. Captain Foster of "City of Flint" saw this and sensed an opportunity. His ship had two whistles. One was shrill; the other one bass like a bull frog. He always carried a good head of steam in the boiler. He pulled the cord to the high pitched whistle. The young gelding pricked up his ears and turned his head away from the docks. The car moved a bit. Evidently the brake was not secured. Immediately Captain Foster released the frog and pulled the high-pitched whistle cord again. The horse started to buck. It was getting to him, so the captain pulled them both at the same time.

Somebody hollered, "Whoa! Whoa! Whoa!"

It was too late. That big gelding took off down South Long Lake Road to the west with that empty trolley like it was a matchbox. In a short distance, the horse-car jumped the steel track. From then on the dust, dirt and gravel stones flew until he came to the first curve in the road. A corner of the car was snagged on a red oak and reduced to kindling, except for the undercarriage and wheels. This panicked the young gelding all the more, with lumber and debris flying all about. At this point in the runaway, he broke loose from the remains of the horse-car. Somebody caught the winded horse at Torrey Road corner. He had shed it all; the car, the beautiful brass trimmed harness and his bondage.

It was understood that there were harsh and salty words exchanged between the two freshwater captains about this runaway — so it was a testy incident in more ways than one.

If this account be true, it would seem that the rivalry over boat passengers on Long Lake became a diabolical business. When queried, Captain Foster could have used the excuse that he only blew the whistles to notify people waiting on the dock that his ship was ready to take them aboard and move out.

Needless to say, this runaway of the horse-car had an equalizing effect on the excursion business on Long Lake.

It Was Sawed

This narrative relates to the recreation of life. It is the game of courtin'. Not today or yesterday, but a hundred years ago. Indirectly, it caused a runaway.

Private courtin' was carried on by horse and buggy. It seems that a young man by the name of Preston, "Pret" for short, was fortunate to have the opportunity to escort the belle of the community to the Wednesday night prayer meeting to hear the parson pray and preach. When endured from the wooden benches, it was a tiresome three-hour service. The only people with back supports were those on benches placed along the outside walls. When compared with modern standards, the lighting was also grossly inadequate. Four coal-oil bracket lamps with mercury reflectors illuminated the rostrum. That was about it, except for a small hanging lamp near the single entrance and a post lamp in the churchyard.

The young people occupied the back seats of the sanctuary and there was nary a complaint from them about the lighting.

Pret and his guest of the evening sat on one of these rear benches. She allowed Pret to hold her hand and to pat her knee several times. As a result, he was looking forward with anxious anticipation to the buggy ride home behind his high-stepping mare.

The meeting finally came to a close. After a few hurried handshakes at the door, Pret and his belle skedaddled out to his buggy. A fancy new buggy robe was meticulously tucked in about her limbs. She made not even a token protest which would have been the proper thing for a virtuous young thing to do.

For once in his life, it appeared that everything was going his way.

He untied the mare and it was, "Git up Molly." They moved forward through the departing crowd slowly and carefully, not wishing to lock wheels with another rig or do anything that would delay their exit. Under the circumstances, when the buggy hit the open road, it was natural for a young buck to attract attention by showing a little class. The best way to do that was with plenty of speed. In those days, there was no accelerator to tromp on, but his mare was the fastest little witch in the township. So Pret gave Molly her head and with some reserve in his voice said, "Go Molly."

She could fly, especially with that light "go meetin'" single seater — and she did.

The singletree snapped, the thills slid right on out of their carriers on her back pad, the loosely held lines slithered through Pret's leather gloves and before a commanding "Whoa," could be shouted, high stepping Molly was well on her way home, minus one fancy buggy and its contents. It was a one horse runaway by command.

Without regard for the consequences, Pret left his lovely sitting in the middle of the road and took off after that mare with his coattails flopping humorously behind him. The pace soon slowed. Darkness covered his embarrassed departure.

A bright moon hung at midnight, by the time he was able to return to the empty buggy, contrite and confused. How could this have happened, he thought to himself. He led Molly by one hand and carried a new singletree in the other. He was too proud to ask anyone for help and definitely on the defensive at this point, until he stumbled on the broken singletree laying in the road. It was the source of his embarrassment and downfall. He rolled it over in his hand, examined it carefully, then shouted to the lonesome moon so loud that it spooked Molly and she almost broke from his grasp again.

"Some smart aleck, some scallywag, some scamp, some scoundrel sawed that singletree almost in two! It did not break, it was sawed. Whoever did the sawing left but a smidgen of wood holding. Just enough to get us in the road, and then that somebody stole my girl. Who was the smart arse?"

Gyp — A Reverse

This is a horse story that will not be endearing to horse lovers. It is also a true recounting of a case of justifiable arson in which strange bedfellows play the lead roles. The time was in the depths of the 1930 Depression. The location, a poverty stricken small farm in mid-Michigan.

I was young then. I thought that we were destitute, but now as I reflect on the past we had everything without knowing it. We were shook-up by the loss of a good horse. There had been only two. Not a team like a few rich farmers owned. Not a pair of horses that would work with a straight evener all day. Not a pair of horses called a team that was of about the same age, weight, conformation and color. No, simply two odd horses that were hitched up together to do the jobs that had to be done on a small acreage. One died. He was Black Doc, nineteen years old and it was his time to go.

It was in the summer of 1931 and he was worth all of twenty-five dollars. That was a fortune. Now we were down to one horse and that was all the power and transportation we had except for a Fordson tractor that had taken to growling inside. In reality, it was a second dead horse, but it did not have to be buried by shovel because it never took to stinking.

The motor on the Fordson ran fine, but with gasoline at nine cents per gallon we could not afford to start it up. There was only one solution. It was to beg, borrow or steal a replacement horse. The first idea worked. My father presented himself to an ominous tall rawboned hawk of a man who presided over the giving and taking in the community as cashier of a local private bank. Very few kind words would you hear spoken among the natives of this banker; occasionally something humorous made the rounds of the party line.

Like the last time he ever went deer hunting. Rawbones was sitting on a stump near a deer run properly attired in a red suit enjoying an Indian Summer day when — Wham! Crack! Lead from a 30-06 lodged deep in the wood about two feet below where he was sitting. Somehow news of this warning miss reached his home community before he did. As far as is known, this was his last deer hunting foray.

However, he was always kind to us and tolerant of our needs. That day he granted us a line of credit not to exceed fifty dollars to purchase a horse, for which in exchange he accepted a chattel mortgage on all the personal property we possessed, which was nothing. He was beat, but he had faith that some day, somehow, we would pay it back plus 5% interest.

Father and I went to call on the only horse jockey in the community. He was unscrupulous as hell, but otherwise a fine fellow. He said that he was expecting us. How come? We didn't tell a soul. He had seventeen horses. Boy! They were worth a lot of money.

We shopped like demons, going over each animal carefully with the jockey. Somehow after two hours of dickering it boiled down to economics. How did he know how much we had to spend? It was embarrassing. We never told anyone. He had some beautiful green-broke three-year-old geldings (broke to halter and lead if you could catch them) for one hundred dollars each. However, all our shopping finally simmered on down to a young fat black mare with scars, priced at forty dollars. The jock said that she had been the last horse out of a sale barn fire in Galesburg, Illinois, in which many others perished. That clinched the deal. This mare had been through a lot. We felt sorry for her and would give her a good home. As small talk on the deal, the jock kept telling us how good the mare was to ride and that we might better ride her into town than to hook her up to a buggy. That suited me fine because any kid would rather ride than drive.

He had what was called an old humpback trailer (made on an old auto frame) which we hitched behind his car and he took us all home. We had hitchhiked and walked over. It was only about nine miles.

Gyp was slick as a dairy barn tomcat and fat as butter. She was about five years old and had not done much hauling because there were no collar marks about her neck or mane. When we got her home, to show off in front of the womenfolk, I jumped on her bare back and with only a rope halter for a rein, rode in a nice easy lope toward the stable door. It was open. She did not respond to whoa! So I had to exit pronto by way of her fat rump. No harm done. She had to be taught to obey a few commands, which could come later. Everybody laughed about how the new mare Gyp had shucked me.

After dad had signed a release to him for the forty dollars against the fifty-dollar line of credit, the jockey reemphasized the care we should use in handling Gyp.

"Now fellows, be careful and easy with her when you first hook her up. She might lead you to believe that she was a wee bit cold-shouldered." He spit out his chewing tobacco, jumped in his car, and soon disappeared up the hill in a cloud of dust headed for the bank with the humpback trailer bringing up the rear.

We did nothing with Gyp, but feed, bed and pet her this first night. Morning brought forth another day with big plans for activity. The wagon was out behind the barn next to the manure pile where old Doc had dropped dead after returning from the field for the last time. Before breakfast we loaded up the wagon. After breakfast there was only one thing to do; throw the harness on the horses and get on with the job. We had been pitching manure on the wagon with forks and unloading it the same way on some clay knobs a spell down the lane.

The new black mare took the pad, collar and harness like a veteran. Out of the stable door we led the horses singly. Once outside, we ran the lines through the spreader rings and snapped them up to their bits, untied the lines from the britchens, drove them around the barn and got them up and over the wagon tongue, snapped up the neck yoke, hooked up the tugs and Dad said, "Get up."

Our remaining old horse leaned into the collar as usual, but the pretty slick new fat mare just stood there chomping on the bit and tossing her head in the morning sun. Then she reared straight up with her front feet pawing the air viciously. Next she began kicking out in all directions with her hind feet. She chipped a splinter off the tongue, rattled the whiffletree first rate and ended up the tantrum by getting both hind legs outside the tugs.

"Whoa, Gyp! Whoa! Do you suppose we have hitched her on the wrong side?" Dad asked. "Maybe she is used to working on the near side," he continued.

"OK," I said. "Let's try the other side. Something, for sure is not to her liking."

It took only a short time to switch her over, by unhooking the tugs, the neck yoke and leading her out and changing the lines. It was no sweat. The old gelding could not have cared less where he worked except he took a healthy nip at her withers as he stumbled over the tongue.

Evidently Gyp did not like the near side as well as the off side.

She laid down right beside the tongue in that sloppy manure the instant Dad said, "Get up Gyp." She went absolutely contrary. We did everything we could think of to get her up and out of that mess. She was ruining our harness. We begged, we teased, we beat her sparingly, unhitched her from the load, took off the collar. Nuthin'. She would not move a muscle. We could not even get her to kick now. She seemed to have gone completely out of gear just like the old Fordson.

There was only one movement within that dormant body. That was with her eyes. Oh, brother! How she could roll up those whites in her eyes. My father was not known as a swearing man but there were some choice new words that I had never heard before practiced around the barnyard that morning. That mare would have made a preacher increase his vocabulary.

Mother heard the commotion and came out. "Why don't you build a fire under her then she will move." That was it, the scars! Somebody, sometime, somewhere had built a fire around that mare to move her. There was no such thing as a horse-barn fire. Dad would not start a fire about her and besides it was too close to our barn. We worked with that mare until dinnertime when mother came back out saying she had some potato soup and corn bread ready. Away we went to wash up for dinner leaving Gyp laying in the slop and rolling the whites of her eyes up at us. A few minutes later from the dinner table, we looked out toward the barn and there she was, eating grass in the yard. What a mess to behold. She must have rolled over and righted herself soon after we left.

The next day after she had dried off, we cleaned her up and rode her back to the horse jockey begging for our money back. We were worse off than ever. In debt forty dollars and still only one horse. After some evasive haranguing, he finally admitted she would not work and allowed us the fifty dollars credit on a tried and true old skin.

Horse trainers will say that we did not know how to handle Gyp. A good horseman told us later that we should have shut off her wind. Well, we didn't dare to stand anywhere near those front hooves. It looked like a sure way to commit suicide. Arson is a crime, and in this case, it would be classified as cruelty to animals.

Courts have at sometime or other, in someway or another, justified to some extent every crime written into the statute. In horse country where breaking horses is one's livelihood, I do not suppose anything would come of it if a straw fire were set about a balky horse to get it to move. In other areas, one would be prosecuted promptly and chastised for life by the public for using a fire to move a horse.

Here in the middle country we did not attempt to solve the problem. We concluded that we had run up against a damn smart mare and the only way she knew how to prove the point was by being balky — besides it could be bad for your blood pressure. A reverse runaway for sure. She ran us.

Maude Gets Hot

Before I move on into the tales of some real horse runaways that extended as far as a mile, let me tell you of a brief one. It is said that it happened on a Hereford Cattle Farm near Belding.

This runaway was positive to some extent. Its course was all of ten feet and also had to do with a stubborn mare. Her name was Maude. She was hitched with a dependable pair of geldings on a grain binder. The field had been opened up only the night before and the first bundles from the outside swath had been picked up out of the standing grain and set up near the fence row. It looked like a great day for cutting wheat, but the driver had sensed that not all was as well as it appeared. Maude would warn you beforehand if she was going to balk, in this way. When the harness was thrown on her she would lay her ears back and look like a mule. That she did.

Sure enough, when the three horses were hitched up to the binder, instead of stepping up into the collar, Maude knelt down on her knees. She turned her head around and "kinda" gazed back over the top of her blinders at the driver with an "I told you so look." This made him angry.

There he was perched high upon the binder seat with the

the cattle is in good rig, by being given access to all the unhusked bundled corn he could eat, these glands may not be visible because of being completely encased in fat. These are the kidneys. While your head is inside the carcass look down. Your view is blocked off by the diaphragm. Extending both ways from the belly opening parallel with the ribs is a border of thin lean muscle which gradually subsides into a veil of taut white tissue.

The butcher makes two quick slashes through the diaphragm and exposes the heart and lungs. The heart is enclosed in yet another sac that holds a small amount of clear fluid.

You are curious. You ask, "What happened to the liver?"

That is a good question. The liver has already taken off. It is under that pile of stomachs and their associates. Here, take a look. There it is, at least twelve pounds or more. The butcher retrieves it from the pile and does some fancy cutting about the ducts until he comes across a fragile appearing sac loaded with what looks like a venomous fluid. It is. It is the gall bladder and contains enough bitterness to render the entire beef inedible if this bile is spread about in vulnerable areas, thus say the old-timers. Bile is thought to have some dubious medicinal value but no one has ever become ill enough to down any of it. However, in cattle, this so-called evil fluid is drained off into the duodenum and is said to aid their digestion.

The liver is trimmed. The heart is secured and trimmed. The lungs are thrown to the dogs. A little washing of capillary blood from the neck about completes the bee, except — the most precise and one of the hardest jobs at a beef butchering bee is yet to come. It takes the strength and skill of several people. One bad slash, and pounds of the best meat in the carcass will be mutilated. It is the halving of the beef. The oxtail is unjointed from the spinal column at the top of the carcass. A bucksaw is best for opening a cut to the first breakaway vertebra. After that it is broadaxed all the way. In the judgment of the head butcher, whosoever misses the mark is disqualified and the most accurate wielder of the broadaxe is awarded the oxtail. It is the source of choice small pieces of meat and has the best joints for soup stock in the entire carcass. Once divided the halves are raised to maximum height allowed by the block and tackle and out of reach of leaping dogs. After the meat sets up or hardens which is usually overnight, it is

EARLY MEAT MARKET
Stocked for the holiday trade.

quartered, trimmed of any foreign material and made ready for consumption.

Mutton and By-Products

There were sheep slaughtering bees in which the yield was lamb and mutton. I will delete the details because it followed closely the procedure of a beef butchering bee. The meat had greater dietary value than either pork or beef and was particularly used by country people with digestive troubles. Mutton fat or tallow was also considered superior to both lard and beef fat. Wool was clipped from the pelts and used the same as the fleeces shorn from the live sheep in springtime. The clipped pelts were salted, cured and used for everything from making a collar pad for a sore-shouldered workhorse to house slippers for the family.

Tar and Ticks

Sheep shearing was usually done at neighborhood bees. The young country boys had input here that was of more than a passing interest. They could not catch ewes and drag them to the shearing platform because the ewes were too large. Boys were not allowed to box and tie fleeces because this job was too particular. As might be surmised, boys were not allowed to stand idly by and watch. They were kept busy another way.

Even an expert manual sheep shearer would nick every animal several times, because of their wiggling and twisting. As soon as a sheep was shorn it was turned over to the boys. Their job was to dab pine tar on every one of those cuts. By the time all of the sheep had been run through this process the boys would be covered with blood, pine tar — and sheep ticks.

It was a common custom to go over to the chicken coop and leg up a half dozen cawing hens and throw them into the pen with the newly shorn flock. The hens would wise up fast. They would start walking the backs of the sheep and pick off the ticks like they would pick earthworms off the lawn after a spring shower.

A person could not handle sheep at shearing time without becoming infested with ticks, especially if he was wearing wool clothing. Sheep ticks do not like humans and they will get off as soon as possible, but they are slow and deliberate. It might take them a couple of days to exit, unless the host made an effort to hunt them down.

The posterior of a full grown sheep tick is by far the largest part of his body. By bringing a goodly amount of pressure to bear with the ends of one's fingers, the tick will pop loud enough to be heard all over a room. A young boy who loved to tantalize his mother and sisters would leave the sheep shed ladened with a healthy supply of ticks. When opportunity presented itself, he would reach into a pocket and sort out a plump tick. A move with his hand toward the neck of one of his sisters would follow. This was feinting that he had picked a tick off from her. Then, much to the amusement of the menfolk, he would pop it.

Connivers

A look-see into poultry butchering was directly the opposite. Country people did get together to kill poultry of all kinds for shipment in barrels by train to the city. The market for poultry and even eggs in the countryside and its villages was very limited because everyone kept poultry regardless of where they lived. The market was in the city. It took cooperative effort between neighbors to prepare a few barrels of iced fowl to roll on the 3:40 p.m. fast train bound for Detroit.

A poultry bee took specialists, too. They were the sticker, the scalder, pluckers, drawers and finishers. The interesting sidelight was not in the work but in the potluck held soon afterwards. The scalder and the pluckers would always get their heads together. The water would somehow become too hot. The feathers would seize and the pluckers would pay no heed. The skin on several chickens would be torn, particularly about the crop and breast. There was no way they would be accepted in the city in damaged condition. They had to be eaten. There was no time or need to do anything but cook them up for the potluck. So it was; the socializing was then done on a full stomach.

The same conniving would work when killing turkeys, ducks, geese or what have you.

Poultry Pluckers

Deviation from the subject of food here, is because of the value of a by-product from ducks and geese. This also ties into this text because there was a double demand for good pluckers. Duck feathers and goose down were country basics and city essentials. Cornhusk and straw mattresses were standard for "pore folk." When one made, acquired or fell heir to a feather tick, he was sleeping high on the "hawg," and never alone. It was an item to be shared.

The feather yield from a poultry butchering that included

ducks and geese was always saved for bedding, but the quality was not the best. They would be wet from the scalding and were difficult to dry without becoming mildewed and musty smelling.

"Good gracious," as Norrie Desmond used to say, "who wants to get up in the morning smelling like a duck?"

Also, pioneer women thought that feathers plucked from live birds gave off a pleasant aroma and that the feathers had more resiliency than those taken from poultry that had been butchered. It was argued that they wore better and lasted longer because the natural oils had not been washed from the feathers in scalding. So there you have it, pro and con. This is also an excellent example of a topic that was used for discussion at a monthly Grange meeting.

So — there were plucking bees. Not everyone could be a participant even though he wanted to. Later this inability to perform was identified by a new word; allergy. This could have been where the term "goose bumps" originated. Minute fuzz from the feathers and especially from the down would cause the plucker's body to break out. Particles of fuzz were also inhaled while working and this further fueled the fires for those who were allergic.

There was yet another element that decimated the pluckers. It was the ideology of reincarnation. During early days, throughout the countryside, many people seriously believed that after death they would return to earth in another physical form, such as a dog, cat, horse, goose or whatever. There was much discussion over religion and specifically reincarnation. There were many of these believers. The last thing in the world many of them would wish to be was a dry plucker. In their way of looking at it there was a humanitarian difference between a wet plucker and a dry plucker. If one pulled feathers wet, it was from a dead fowl that had already given up his life for humanity and his soul had already passed on to a new body. Dry pluckers yanked, pulled and stripped feathers and down from live poultry and it was painful to the "pullee." Reincarnates did not relish this possible torturing of their ancestors. To be a dry plucker one had to be callous. Most early settlers were not. They were meek and mild because of the uncertainty of life in those days. Their close association with nature fostered an attitude of humbleness. Good dry pluckers, consequently, were not in surplus. Sometimes it was difficult to get a bee organized. Once it was set up the details became fuzzy, so following is only a rough outline of the actual event.

A plucking bee was a fluffy affair run by the strong-willed women of the community. The women were always in poultry and the funds or other assets accrued were theirs to do with as they pleased. This is why the poultry in the barnyard was sometimes better cared for than the kids in the house.

The ducks and geese were caught after dark the night before they were to be plucked and placed in crates. Come morning, they were loaded on a light wagon with a spring seat and before the sun was too high, off went the wife and children with an ample potluck basket of food to some neighbor's steading for the annual plucking bee. The timing depended on the weather. The quality of late spring weather brought on the moulting season. When the ducks and geese began to lose their winter feathers about the farmyard, it was time to hold the bee. One of the men said that these plucking bees didn't make any sense and that the work could have just as well been done at home. The women disagreed. They would not admit it to the menfolk in so many words, but the real reason was so that the women could get together and talk—yes! Gossip! It was good for the soul after a long confining winter.

"Matilda's children have all come down with chicken pox and she won't be able to get away today. Poor thing. Do you know that this very plucking bee was the only day she had away from home last year, by herself, mind you."

"The schoolmarm is being courted by at least three hired men in the neighborhood and they all chew tobacco. You know she is boarding with us this month. Every night a different one walks her home. My husband Elmer says that as soon as the weather gets a bit warmer they won't be walking her straight to our place, but will be stopping under that big sycamore tree down by the spring. When that starts, he's going to begin hitching up Old Bess every night to go fetch her home by himself. He doesn't have time to stop right in the middle of spring work and go looking for another teacher for the district. He is the moderator of the school board. Well, do you know what I told that man of mine?"

"Elmer," I said, "that getting elected to the school board has plumb gone to your head. I've read most of the words in that school law book they gave you and I can't find a thing about the moderator being the guardian of young school teachers. If she should come sick every morning so that she couldn't teach that is no business of yours, except you would have to hire another teacher with the approval of the other two board members. You betcha I got him out of that idea in a hurry. I can read that law book better than he can. Don't tell anybody. He only went to the fourth grade."

This is a fair to middlin' sample of the gossip.

It was a field day for all the able-bodied neighborhood women that could stand the plucking, both mentally and physically. It was mean work but still recreation and a change of pace because of the socializing.

The last statement about sums up the reason for holding a bee of any type, except that there were many of these jobs that could not be accomplished within a family. Plain brawn and usually experienced assistance was needed. It also was a training ground for the young people within these families. By this method they became qualified to go out and establish homes of their own with that girl they met across the hair sorting table at the hog butchering bee.

Barn Building

A barn raising was looked forward to as a colossal event not only for the family involved but for the entire community. It was a social thing. In truth, it was all fun. The backbreaking labor was never taken into consideration. A series of local bees were usually held as a means of assisting the owner in preparing the materials to be used for the main event.

The actual raising of the barn was the culmination or climax rather than the beginning, as those who are not informed might be led to believe.

Any decisions made were family decisions. Families lived, worked and played as a unit. Once the die was cast, it was full

TIME OUT FOR THE PHOTOGRAPHER
This barn raising was not over. The ridge pole was yet to be raised plus the supporting rafters. Ninety people are in this picture.

steam ahead. The children would walk to school the next day and spread the word.

"We are going to have a barn raising. Will ya-all come?"

The news was carried home to other families by their children. Immediately it became the first statement in conversation wherever people met, often by stopping their rigs in the middle of the road. Within a week the good news had spread for twenty miles by word of mouth, which was the only means of communication.

"Philander McLain is going to build a new barn, come next fall."

"Gracious me," the wife would reply, "that's less than a year hence. They will have to hustle."

Thus, the word was out. In response to the word came felicitations, congratulations, offers of help, suggestions, expressions of sympathy and solicitations by craftsmen for possible use of their particular talents, etc. The project had to be squeezed into the crowded routine of daily and seasonal tasks. This was accomplished by stepping up the pace and stretching the hours of the day. The day began earlier and lasted longer into the evening.

It was a family undertaking and there were decisions to be made.

"Dad, say Dad! Where are we going to put the barn?"

Philander would answer after some heavy pondering, "I guess we better call Ma and your sisters and go out on the buzz pile and figure that one out. They should have more to say 'bout that than us, seeing as how they will be doing chores and slopping the "hawgs" all summer while we menfolk are in the field."

Family conferences settled the major points. They would have a south barnyard extending to the creek. There would be a rock foundation with the southwest corner anchored on that grey granite boulder. The horse stalls would be in the corner closest to the house and that was the way it went. There was a well-thought-out reason to back-up each determination, and that is the manner in which each steading was put together and in turn, the entire countryside.

The amount of folding money that would be transferred from one person to another in a barn building project, during this era, was minimal. Barter, trading work and community bees were the method of exchange. Hard cash was scarce. Everybody traded the same way. A nest egg was not needed. All that was needed was the desire and a strong body.

There were two kinds of barn raisings. One was where an all-out professional effort was made. A craftsman, called a framer, was hired and he made all preparations for a large one-day event. Every piece of material needed would be on the grounds down to the last roof board and shingle. The bents would be framed and supported on blocks awaiting the pike poles of a hundred or more strong-armed men. The mortised joints fit. The pins were driven by young daredevils standing on eight inch beams with forty-pound beetles clutched in their hands while thirty feet off the ground. It was "heave ho, men" and a new barn would come into being.

"Easy men, now all together. Good! Hold her right there.

Ebner, toss him a pin." They continued until all was in place, including the roof.

The other barn raising event would need help only in raising the bents. The owner with his sons and hired hands would later lay the sub-floor, put on the siding, use a froe to split the shingles, etc. The barn dance would be held when all was completed. At such time, all those who helped to raise the frame would be present with other guests for a high old time. It was usually held on a Saturday night or on a convenient holiday.

The first visible action, on the part of the landowner, would be in providing drainage for the site. The tools used would be a team, walking plow, and both a board and a slip scraper plus some lazy-back shovels. Once the building site was selected it was rearranged by landscaping so that water would get away from the foundation quickly. The barnyard had to be well drained so that livestock would stand high and dry during all kinds of weather.

The most important part of a new barn was the wall. There were two ways to go. This foundation could be provided by hauling large deadheads in from the fields and laying the sills directly on top of them. This was a floating foundation that would move, rise and fall, with the freezing and thawing. These large rocks had to be so aligned that the weight of the barn and its eventual contents were distributed evenly. This was a painstaking job. Usually neighbors were consulted.

The other type of foundation was a chinked stone wall built up to a desired height to support the building from forty-two inches below ground level. This was considered a safe depth and was below the frost line. Thus there was not supposed to be any movement because of the effects of the weather. It was permanent and thought to be the best of the two styles. However, the labor was many times over that required to build the barn on a floating foundation and the skill of a stonemason was necessary.

There were yet many other tasks to be performed before the barn raising bee took place.

Logs were selected on the stump during the previous fall or before sap began to rise in the trees early the same year in which the barn was to be built. Trees were girdled and allowed to air cure while standing. There was much contention, and lively discussion about this timber-seasoning method while chawing tobacco around the pot-bellied stove at the country store in the wintertime.

About this time the owner would call in a framer for consultation. A framer would review the dimensions and come up with a complete bill of materials needed right off the top of his head. Perhaps the two of them would even go out into the woods and size up the trees that had been selected for the new barn. If they were a little short — what did they do? They borrowed a few trees from a neighbor. Trees were one thing that most every early settler had in surplus.

"Sure, help yourself Philander. When I raise a barn you can pay me back. Reckon it will be ten years."

The trees were cut and either broadaxed or hauled to a mill. Out came sills, posts, purlin plates, braces, rafters, joists, flooring, siding, roof boards, etc. — "the whole ball of wax."

The sills were placed on the wall and mortised. The floor joists were set in the sill and temporarily pinned. Flooring was laid over the joists more as a worktable than anything else. Nothing was finalized at this stage because there was more curing and shrinking of the wood to take place.

The upright sections of framing which included both ends and several bents along the length of the barn were laid out. They were all assembled laying flat on the ground.

This was precision work. Everything had to fit, even to the rafters. The professional framer was usually called back to oversee the raising.

After careful consideration, a date would be set for the barn raising. Every last soul within convenient driving distance would be notified, invited and expected to show up.

This meant strong men with pike poles from 12 to 18 foot long, good strong country women who could cook all day and dance all night, every young person of "courtin' " age and the whole kit and caboodle of youngsters.

There was no event under the stars that communities attended en masse like they did barn raisings.

When a social event was held at a church only the parishioners of that particular sect attended. School doings were usually limited to those people who resided in that one country school district but a raising was for everybody — even the hired men and the hired girls — the schoolmarm, "Oh, ain't she pretty" — the minister (a pike pole never caressed his hands) — all the business people, "iffin it was nye to a village" — hucksters passing through — gandy dancers — tramps — musicians — and the saloon keeper with his fast team and buckboard loaded to the gills with kegs to supplement the homemade applejack.

More important than liquid refreshments was the food. It took a mountain of food to feed the multitude, so assembled. The feast began about high noon. The eating never stopped until "three o'clock in the morning," when the swinging on the corner, clogging and stomping ceased because of sheer exhaustion.

There was another demand for nourishment. It was for the horses. Fifty to seventy-five horses would be tied to trees, fence posts, hitching rails and fancy cast iron tie blocks. Some of the more affluent would fetch along their own hay and a nose bucket of oats, but most of them would depend upon their host's feed supply for their horses. That many hay burners would about clean out a small haymow in the fifteen hours they were on the premises, to say nothing about the hole they would make in the oat bin. Most of the drivers made it a practice to take off out of their own driveways with their horses hungry. They always figured that a hungry horse was a fast horse and he would have all day to eat at the expense of the host, once they arrived at the site of the barn raising.

A barn raising was an institution. Few barns were exactly the same. Their style was dictated by the needs and the character of the owners. Consequently, barns and other buildings throughout the countryside, that have outlived their owners, preserve for present viewers individualities of the past.

Corn Husking and the Mating Game

Barns were kept neat and clean because of plain country pride. Because they were presentable and large, they also were used for social activities. Common work-related bees were held within barns. Usually when the labor was completed the socializing began. There were some exceptions to this rule. One was the annual winter husking bee in which socializing stood on equal footing with the work. Let me explain to you why it was considered as being of equal importance.

Acreages of cleared land were small and every bit of fodder that could be gleaned from them was stored in the barn to feed the livestock during the off season. Hand planted fields of corn were cut with a corn knife, bound into bundles and shocked in the field as soon as the kernels on the ears dented. These stalks contained a lot of natural plant juices and were very nutritional. They were left in a shock in the field until they dried down. They called it passing through a "sweat." The shocks were hauled to the barn and put under cover as soon as possible after cider making time.

It was customary to place a keg of cider (containing the proper accouterments) in the mow first. Time and the insulating effects of the stalked corn piled on top and all about the keg imparted a flavor to the end product that was made available by no other process known to that day or since.

The resulting corned applejack served as the pot of gold at the base of the rainbow when the husking was finished.

Well-known Laurie Brunson said this about a husking bee, "They'd come in an shuck m'corn, sing and have the best time. You've never seen such a good time as they had! I wish you could go to a corn shuckin' sometime."

Most of the participants were young or at least single, except for the farmer and his wife who owned the corn. No money changed hands for shucking. In exchange, the young people expected plenty of food throughout the day with the privilege of having an unchaperoned party which lasted well into the night or even until the next morning—all in the barn.

During the day any young man who shucked out a red ear was entitled to run down, catch and kiss the girl of his choice. As the day matured, the girls were not so hard to catch. The more husking he did, the greater his chances were of finding red ears. Girls shucked too. Not as vigorously as the boys, but occasionally a girl would find a red ear. This she would hide within her clothing until such time as she could secretly reveal it to the young man of her choice. He would grab the ear and proceed to collect the premium amid a swirl of cornstalks, squeals and giggles. If the pair was sufficiently amorous, they might lose themselves in the fluffy pile of husks that were always separated from the stalks and ears.

Once the keg of corned applejack was located the socializing began in earnest. There would be music and dancing and plenty of pairing off.

No decent young woman was allowed to go to a husking bee unless her parents considered her to be of marriageable age, sufficiently skilled in the culinary arts and able to maintain a home of her own. When it appeared that the time had arrived for the young people, to strike out on their own as judged by the family elders, a husking bee was a perfect example of the vehicle used to grease the skids.

CHAPTER IX

COUNTRY CONTRAPTIONS AND COMPLICATIONS

S INCE THE TELEPHONE was first introduced to local subscribers in about 1903, the people of the Great Lakes area have adopted it for their very own. Congenial people are apt to socialize via the wire more than the average. People who are more frugal, both with their time and money, use the telephone more than others. This in turn leads into a variance of topics. Because of these recreational and economic benefits, a Scottish immigrant, Alexander Graham Bell, inventor of the telephone in 1876, and his disciples have always been regarded as extra special by the inhabitants of this fresh water area.

Party Line Telephone

The country party line was a primitive apparatus when compared to modern day telecommunications. It was the source of

CENTRAL SWITCHBOARD

A three unit switchboard as used at the Davison, Michigan exchange. One of these consoles would be sufficient for a small country town and the surrounding community.

much humor, gossip and some business. Perhaps it would be enlightening to explain briefly what a country party line telephone was and how it operated. It has not been over the hill very long but long enough so that most of the people now using a telephone have never heard of it. A good descriptive beginning would be to say that nothing about it was automatic. The heart of the operation was the central switchboard that was manned around the clock. It was located in a private home rather than in an office. The control center was completely manual. It might contain as many as a hundred circuits or lines. Some of these country lines might have as many as twenty subscribers. There were only a few private lines. These would be doled out carefully to the most important people and to the essential businesses. There would be a few outside circuits for long distance calls, but by far it was a local enterprise.

Subscribers on a party line might be billed each quarter of a year at the rate of $1.25 per month plus the long distance calls that were made from his number. Each subscriber was assigned a signal ring. There were no numbers, per se. When his presence was wanted at the wall telephone installed in his home or business, the central operator would manually ring his signal. For example, it might be one long and three shorts. The eight or ten other subscribers on the same line also heard the ring of one long and three shorts on line seventeen. They all knew each other's ring by heart, and this ring was for the Widow Prosser's place. Not wanting to miss prime gossip in the making, everyone who was available and heard the one long and three shorts, made a mad dash for the receiver and cupped a hand tightly over the mouthpiece to shut out all possible incoming domestic noises.

Sometimes so many people would take down their receivers to listen that the interference would make it impossible for the talking parties to carry on their conversation.

When a receiver was taken off the hook, the release of weight of same put the contraption into gear, or in other words, caused a contact to be made. It plugged in the nefarious listener, but not without warning the people already on the line by sounding a pronounced click. This sound would draw uncomplimentary remarks from the people wishing to talk. These remarks were orbital in character and ranged from slander to humor. It was also an excellent time in which to unload on your neighbor who had been cutting cross-lots on your land. He was not supposed to be listening to your conversation but you knew that he was, so this was a golden opportunity to give him a piece of your mind, indirectly.

"Harry, you know that good-for-nothin' that borrowed my posthole digger and never brought it back, the fellow that lives across the road and down a spell? Well! His horses got out last night. They came up to our place and trampled our garden and ate all the sweet corn. Now, if he doesn't come up here, like a man that he isn't, and pay for the damages I am going to turn a bill over to an attorney for collection. Harry, they are a family of nincompoops. They have kids over there that are four years old and still in diapers. They can't raise what they have and now have another one on the way. It looks like a downright case of child neglect. All this neighborhood needs is a couple more backsliders

SUBSCRIBER'S WALL TELEPHONE

The new method of communicating with the outside. It would bring help in
an emergency and trouble if you were looking for it.

like him and we are on the way to hell on a handcar. Oh, his wife
is not to blame, but I think he has something missing from his
upper story."

And so the derogatory statements would be forthcoming as long
as the listener remained on the line. When the listener would get
so mad that he could not stand it any longer he had two choices.
To open up and reply to slanderous remarks would be to reveal
his identity and start a wholesale retort. The other option would
be to hang up, which is what the talkers were wanting him to do
in the first place.

Party lines were "tailor made" for country women. As they
matured and became grandmothers their techniques improved.
Their tactics depended on conditions and upon their personalities. Personalities that were warped by the hardships and impov-
erishment of their times. One of few channels available for them
to use to vent their pent-up feelings and to serve as a safety valve
was the telephone. Idle talk and malicious gossip were their bag

and they were properly identified as wags by the men. Suppose there were a couple of old country women on your party line passing back and forth choice bits of gossip and you wanted to get them off to make an important business call. You listened a bit until you could identify them and pleasantly asked them if you could have the line to call the blacksmith, Charlie Dunkle.

"My best mare Roxy has thrown a shoe. I can't work her on the sulky plow like she is. It looks like winter is coming on fast and I want to finish that fall plowing."

"A likely story," one wag retorts. "It must have taken you a long time to come up with that fancy excuse. We have heard them all. We were not born yesterday. We have only been on this line for two hours and pay our $1.25 monthly toll same as you do. Why don't you get off the line yourself and go back to your whittling because we want to talk about you next. What we have to say might burn your ears."

The central (operator) was a power in these small communities. If she liked you and you were tolerable when the phone was out of order she would do most anything for you at any hour of the day or night. On the contrary, if you did not pay your telephone bill on time, complained about poor service and were obnoxious, you might as well have your phone disconnected because she would not put out a fire call for you, if your barn was burning.

The apparatus at the central switchboard was wired up so that by throwing a master switch the operator could activate all thirty lines (or whatever) simultaneously. This was used to inform the community of various emergency situations as quickly as possible. Calling for help to fight a fire was the primary use. Twelve rings in rapid succession brought everyone to the telephone on the run for directions to the fire. The central operator would open all circuits and make an announcement as to the name of the unfortunate family whose property was on fire and the location. The fastest transportation was by horseback, but it was difficult to carry a bucket for fighting fire while astride a galloping horse. Most people would throw the harness on their fastest driver, hitch him to their fastest rig and pick up neighbors enroute. If it was a serious fire, the operator would repeat the all circuits alarm.

The same notification system was also used for lesser calamities, but never the twelve rings. They were reserved for a fire, exclusively. Ten rings might be used to inform the subscribers of the death of a prominent citizen. Eight was often used to advertise a church supper, box social or even a chivaree.

A subscriber (or a voting member, if it was a mutual company) on a party line could ring any other subscriber on that particular line without going through the overworked central switchboard. The signal of two long rings was usually reserved, by custom, for notification to all of an emergency within that immediate neighborhood. These emergencies would not concern the entire countryside, but were important to those living locally.

Two long strong rings, "This is Sadie Shaw, our bull has busted the barnyard board fence, the men are on the back forty mowing and they cannot hear me ringing the dinner bell for help. He has chased my Johnny up that Snow Apple tree and he is pawing and bellowing around the roots of that tree like a spring tornado. I need someone to help me let the heifer out of her pen to calm him down 'til the menfolk come up for supper."

In spite of serious limitations the party line telephone system was a definite improvement over the ringing of dinner bells, yelling across the valley, Indian smoke signals or beating upon a hollow log, as we reach back into primitivistic life.

The Drummer's Role

Because of the unending demands for strenuous physical labor to keep body and soul united, the early settlers were always on the alert for short cuts to arrive at an end, labor saving ideas and lastly, new inventions.

Drummers, entrepreneurs and con men out for the fast buck literally flooded the hinterlands with their products. The people were gullible. The traveler did not have to possess much sales ability to make a good return for his efforts.

Many items were merchandised that fell short of their promised goal. Much culling of new inventions took place. A hundred years later when I came along this was still going on and it continues even today. Allow me to share with you some fine points on a few items I happened to use and skin my knuckles on, among other things.

I have no intention of downgrading all the early labor saving implements that were invented for use in agriculture. Still, I think that it is of importance to share with posterity some of the unique moments of my association with a few of the more prominent machines.

The McCormick Binder

Cyrus McCormick invented the reaper in 1831 and by the time I ceased being the gleam in my father's eye, it was called the binder, with an optional newfangled swinging contraption called the bundle carrier. Other accessories were a set of trucks that mounted under the tongue to take the weight of the machine off from the horses' necks, and a combination tin toolbox, whip socket and oil-can holder mounted under the drivers seat.

Three good horses could swing a seven foot cut for half a day at a good clip, if it was cool. During a hot afternoon the driver could go to shocking up what he had cut in the morning, and let the horses swat flies under a tree, or put on a fresh team and keep that bull wheel a rolling. Yep, that bull wheel was the source of all power. It drove the pitman that was connected to the cutter bar, the rollers that drove the three canvasses and the almighty important unpredictable knotter that tied the twine about the bundle of grain.

One time my grandfather had a hired hand who was an excellent teamster but a poor machinist. The hand was chomping at the bit wanting to show everyone that he could cut ten acres of wheat a day without hanging the horses' hides on the fence. Every time he came around the field to where we were shocking bundles, "Gramps" would stop him to rest the horses and to look the binder over. This hand did not know what an oil can was intended for. He was all speed and hell on horses.

At one stop he had a complaint. "You know Willie, this cutter

THE GRAIN BINDER
This one lacks a bundle carrier. Note the fly nets on the horses.

bar just gets lower and lower on me. I have the lever up in the last notch and the knives sometimes run in the dirt." "Gramps" looked over the situation.

It was that "dad gum" bull wheel. The driver had hit too many rocks and ditches going too fast, trying to make the ten acres a day. That drive wheel which normally was forty inches in diameter had been reduced by slam-bang compaction to a ball of scrap iron about one half that height. It was still rotating, doing a job, but in a much smaller circle. The hired hand did not cut the ten acres that day or the next. It was a major repair job. Forge welding was not possible. It required a new wheel.

There were all sorts of controls on this binder. One was a foot trip pedal which controlled the bundle carrier. When the knotter tied a bundle it was expelled down the side of the shield that covered the bull wheel toward the ground. Earlier binders strung bundles along the ground helter-skelter. With the bundle carrier, they could be dumped in rows as you cut around and around the field in bunches of six to eight. However, there was no catch, lock, spring or other resistance of any kind to hold that heavy load of bundles from dumping, except for the pressure of the driver's foot encased in sort of a stirrup on that pedal. Your leg would get so tired that you thought you had lost it for sure before the job was done.

The real "wing ding" of that McCormick was the knotter. It was as tempermental as a Fordson Tractor. The variables that spawned its intemperance were numerous, such as the twine being twisted, too thick or too thin; the driver not keeping the butt lever in proper adjustment for the changing length of the straw; thistles or other coarse weeds winding about the needle; straw too tough or dry; the knotter slipping a cog and going out of time or even a rabbit or snake becoming impaled on the needle. I have heard modern farmers curse the knotter on a hay baler. They were born a century too late to get in on this main event. The main event they missed was the knotter on an early McCormick grain binder. The best tool the operator could have was a sharp jackknife. Twine, green weeds, damp straw all in turn would have to be cut away during a day's work with this labor saver. Many farmers were impaled upon the needles of those early McCormicks. There was a warning that said, "Place binder out of gear before working with knotter"—but they would never take time to do it—too busy—all hurry up. If the knotter was tripped and a horse took a step reaching for a bite of grain, so as to move the bull wheel, up came the needle, quick as you could say scat, and through the muscle of an arm or the palm of one's hand. It was geared high. One could not react fast enough to get out of its way.

The driver was perched on a slotted cast iron seat that was molded to fit the universal male buttocks, but it never did. He never seemed to conform. He was a misfit. This was a place where a sheep pelt came into heavy use. There were no springs, no rubber tires. The driver vibrated until he gave up and let his teeth chatter, especially if one was traveling crossways of the way the field was drilled.

In front of the driver was a pair of footrests, one of which was never used because one foot was always stuck in the bundle carrier stirrup. The lines that he drove the horses with were always in his hands, except when he was doing one of his juggling acts. The juggling was necessary when he was required to adjust one or more of several levers. The most trying one to move was the bundle butt adjustment lever which lay across the top of the binder to his right. It was a piece of strap iron with notches in it. The handle was made by turning the strap iron a quarter turn after heating it white hot in the forge. When the straw was short, the driver brought it toward him and when the straw was long, he went the opposite direction. This caused the twine to be tied in the middle of the sheath. When the straw was long and the grain was rolling up between the canvasses at a rapid clip, it was almost impossible to pull that lever back when there was short grain in the offing.

The only way the cutter bar could be adjusted for height was by raising or lowering the bull wheel and the outer table canvas wheel. Directly in front of the driver a bit above the foot rests were two stubby levers. One of these was to adjust the tilt of the table and cutter bar and the other was to control the height of the reels. These levers were so short they were counterfeits. They gave the driver no leverage. They were simply gut pullers and caused a bushel of trouble in the grain fields. It was not uncommon for a driver to be struggling with the pair of gut pullers (if you moved one to a different notch they both had to be adjusted) and to drop his lines. Before you could say "Whoa!" the lines, one or both, would be wound up in the canvas rollers and be pulling your horses severely right or left. Never would they be pulled back on their haunches because both lines were never pulled equally.

The usual result here was a runaway, which was a common occurrence especially if you were working green broke mustangs. One harvest our family had a good farmhand. His name was Ed S-shu-mor-ee. Never did know how to spell his last name because he had a severe speech impediment and that was the way it sounded. All the men in the family were shocking grain because that was considered of more importance than running the binder, especially if a rain was coming. The very thing I have mentioned happened to Ed. In his struggles with the two handfuls of levers, Ed dropped one line. It gave the horses a quick jerk, the line broke, and they were off to where they pleased. Ed was a good horseman. He stayed on the seat clutching the stubby levers for dear life. Where the horses pleased was over in a hollow under a piss elm tree. Somehow those four tough mustangs were short on communication. They did not have their directions synchronized. They hit the elm shade they were aiming for, but three of them went to the off side. This cartwheeled the binder around the tree and the impact tossed Sh-shu-mor-ee up into some low branches. He was unhurt but very excited, which is the worst thing that can happen to one with a speech impediment.

Nobody could understand a thing he said for a week. The binder was wrecked. A new one only cost $126.00 and grain was about as much per bushel as it is at this writing, only it took more manual labor to gather it in.

Regardless of my sometimes humorous and critical personal observations, farmers of the Great Lakes Watershed are forever grateful to Cyrus McCormick for placing his reaper in the crack of the door that finally opened wide and introduced the industrial revolution to agriculture.

Model 101 Corn Picker by Deere

If you were to place the position of number one on an agricultural crop it would have to be placed on corn. In the beginning, it was a hand job from the time seed was dropped into the soil until it was placed on the food table or used to feed livestock. Logically, much attention was given to eliminating this hard manual labor.

Improvements in methods and machinery soon brought us to the mechanical harvesting of corn. This was a far cry from the husking bee, but the transition consumed fewer years than most of us would like to admit.

THEY SOLD THE HORSES

A McCormick Binder of later design is teamed up with a Fordson that does not runaway — only balks. It took an extra man and gasoline but no oats.

John Deere, from the time he developed the first steel mold-board plow, was an innovator. He was quick to grasp new concepts. Sometimes too quick, or I might add, placed them on the market before proper field testing. So it was with his infamous 101 Corn Picker.

It was built to mount on most standard two or three-plow-size row-crop tractors. By row-crop I am referring to the narrow front-end type of iron horse power plant. Of course, they were especially manufactured to fit John Deere Model A and Model B Tractors. They were useable on other makes of tricycle type farm tractors by securing an adapter kit. It was said by company block men that any red-blooded farm boy could mount one of these contraptions onto his tractor in seven minutes. Actually it was

Complete View of No. 101 Corn Picker with Tractor (Manufactured 1941-1947)

101 NEVER STOOD FOR A THING
It was a machine that could not be aimed like a gun.

much closer to seven hours. It was one and a half tons of malleable and sheet iron mounted on one lonesome wheel. John Deere slipped a big cog right there. In all of God's creation I do not think there was ever a more difficult piece of machinery to maneuver about, either by itself or when attached to its host tractor.

The number 101 never stood for a thing because it picked one row at a pass, except it could have meant by way of warning, that it was only good for 101 rows. The length of the rows would have been irrelevant.

All the "heft" was on the left side of the tractor, once it was mounted. A corn wagon to receive the ears from the picker elevator was attached to a drawbar built into the picker. This was supposed to have some counterbalancing effect. It had none, except when the wagon was heavily loaded, which was seldom.

With dry footing, the side draft could be compensated for by keeping one's right foot on the wheel brake. This would bring the front end of the tractor about so it could be aimed down the corn row. If the corn rows were crooked there was not much of any place to aim. Shortly, one would smell something burning. It would be a hot brake; tomorrow you could count on being in the brake relining business. You had to have a good brake, at least on one side, to hold her straight.

So much for dry footing. Suppose there had been a rain, some snow or a bit of ice. Suppose that in the process, the ground had softened so that the outrigger wheel sunk in a couple inches. If any of these weather conditions prevailed (and they are not uncommon in the fall season), how do you think the front end of that tractor would have reacted? I will tell you. It would have made a half-moon turn in spite of all the operator could do to prevent it. Few rows of corn are planted in that pattern. It was enough to make you reach in your jacket pocket for that trusty husking peg and a pinch of snuff and go at the job by hand.

The only way to harvest a corn crop with a J.D. 101 was to plan on supplementary assistance. The field would require ten shoats per acre or perhaps it would have been best to start with the hogs and leave the 101 in the shed.

Fiery Fordson

The Fordson was an early farm tractor concocted to replace two teams of horses and take the drudgery out of making a living for the eighty acre farmer. It was a wonderful dream that did not quite materialize. It did not develop to the aspired heights because of mechanical inadequacies, but it accomplished a first. It was the first machine to introduce the element of stress to the peaceful countryside. As the years have rolled by these stressful situations that materialized matured into humorous memories. At this writing farming is still one of the top ten most stressful occupations.

This beast of burden was not a junker. It was not a disgrace to

FORDSON TRACTOR
*A good view of the front wheels, the armstrong starter and scars in the
radiator core from the buck sheep's goring.*

its namesake. The tractor was just plain tempermental. It was as
if it were programmed into a negative human disposition. It was
composed of pig iron, a small percentage of steel, some copper
and a bit of brass. Let's put it this way. It was vulnerable to
misuse and had the ability to reciprocate. Taking the front end
first, as you were walking around this battleship grey culprit, you
barked your knee on the extended hand crank. Yes, the crank to
turn the engine. Yes, to start this horse of iron. This was one of
many very unreliable parts of this tractor.

This crank extended to the engine through an opening below
the radiator shell. A spring was slipped over the inner end of this
crank so that you had to exert considerable inward pressure at the
same time as you tried to spin her. The inner end was drilled so a
three-eighths pin was inserted at right angles to engage some
notches that were recessed back inside of a small flat belt pulley,

that drove the large radiator cooling fan. After a couple of hours of steady hand cranking, which was about par, it was difficult to get that pin to hang into those notches because of the lubrication furnished by the sweat that had run down your arm. So — the pin skittered out of its notch and you on the business end of the crank went into a heap on the terra firma much to the amusement of whomever was watching. About this time you had arrived at the point of impatience, where it was no joking matter.

That crank had another booby trap. It was the spark. You see, there was no battery, no alternator or generator, but to provide the fire, there was a super hot or more likely a cold, cold magneto apparatus bolted to the flywheel that was located deep in the bowels of this beast of stress. The control for its spark of life was mounted on the steering post under the steering wheel along with the throttle lever. The setting of this spark lever was not a mathe-matical or engineering decision. Why so much care in the set of the spark? Because, the setting of the spark was the sum total. If it happened to be in a notch coinciding with the disposition of the engine it would fire off. If not the cranker would fire off into the great blue beyond and land on his arse. Only one more comment on the advance or retarding of the spark. It never would fire properly two days in a row from the same notch. We would try to back it into a corner. We tried all the fundamentals like regulat-ing it according to the humidity, barometric pressure or tempera-ture. We toiled with those critters for ten years and never did come up with the why. Why? Two to one it would buck or kick versus firing up. So the odds were that you would lose your touch and your temper. Thus the stress.

As you stepped away from this armstrong engine starter you whacked your shin on the extended crank handle once again. Ouch! It drew your attention to the fragile unprotected copper radiator core. No fins, grill or guard.

A neighbor was raising a new span of horses by the way of a half-sister pair of fillies. They were cavorting about the inside barn lot. The Fordson was stalled there while hot and it abso-lutely refused to blast off again until all the components cooled off. Neighbor Nelson spun the crank until his wife rang the dinner bell. When he came back out after dinner for the second round with the battleship grey dum-dum, it had not moved. It was still there, but something had changed. Yes! That was it. Water. The Ford Son of a B — was sitting in a pool of water. Nels was teed off, that was for sure. He hurried around in front and there it was. A hole, right through the radiator! A perfect imprint made by a small horse's hoof had shoved a whole section of beautiful soft copper radiator core right through so that it was up against the fan blades. He glanced over at that pair of yearling fillies. They just stood in the corner of the lot swishing flies.

There was another local incident about a couple of otherwise highly regarded boys who got to playing bullfight with their unemployed Rambouillet buck sheep. There was an expanse of several months during the year when his services were not needed. To be more factual, they were not even wanted.

Consequently, the ram's temperament became untenable. His heavy ribbed horns were formidable. I have seen a Rambouillet buck sheep rout a herd of cattle from their favorite shady grove and drive them out into the noonday sun. The most amusing encounter I ever witnessed was between an experienced buck and a cocky Banty rooster. When there is an animal of this tempera- ment around a steading, the boys will never pass him by without irritating him. The possibilities are unlimited. They used a horse blanket or old burlap bag and soon became first-class barnyard toreadors. That was the setting at Nelson's soon after he had replaced the radiator that had suffered from the telltale filly hoof print. The fine wool buck sheep chased those boys all over the lot mostly from one small building to another. They would dodge into a doorway and shut the door in his face. Bang! They would no more than reach security when he would be there. One got too brave and was caught by the buck out in the middle of the yard and he had to shinny up the bell pole. The buck figured he was a quitter, nothing but a cheap ding-a-ling and he was getting hotter and madder by the second.

There stood the Fordson. For a distraction and to rescue his buddy from the bell pole, the other boy mounted the gas tank on that tractor like he was riding a horse bareback. He yelled and screamed insults at the ram. It worked. As a decoy, the boy astride the stress buggy was just too good. He stopped pawing at the pole and with only two leaps smacked where the taunting boy's midsection should have been. It moved. It was pliable. His head was soon wet. The Rambouillet tried to back off for another hit. He couldn't. He was held fast. A horn was imbedded in a mass of new copper. Nels was not the least bit forgiving. After the woodshed penalities were paid, Nelson laced three oak 2×4's across that radiator in an act of self-preservation. Returning to the Fordson proper—

As you stepped clear of the extended crank handle and took your eyes off that vulnerable radiator you came to the right front wheel. This was the furrow wheel. This double band of steel riveted together in the middle to form a ridge, was all right. The spokes were tough. You could run "agin" and over a sizable rock that would unroot your teeth and the steel in that front wheel would not even quiver. The trouble with the front wheels were the bearings. The furrow wheel, at times, would wobble like a drunken sailor. This was the sign that the bearing had cut out. Not until this happened would the driver know anything was amiss. When plowing, the front axle would be on an angle because the right front wheel would be six to eight inches lower than the land wheel. As the wheel in the furrow turned, the rim would pick up dirt, sand and stones. This material would be carried to the top of the wheel from where it would casually drift down on and into that bearing. The bearing was supposed to be protected from this transgression by a flimsy tin shield. The soil soon ground the shield out. One soon tired of replacing bearings, hubs and dirt shields. Nels' oldest son was a tinkerer, not a buck teaser. He had messed in the grease and dirt long enough with that down in the furrow front wheel. He bolted a sort of a runner to the spokes of that wheel so it could not turn. It would just slide along in the damp soil at the bottom of the furrow.

"If it doesn't turn it, it can't cut out nuthin.' " That was common sense and good thinking.

The actual runner was handmade from a section of a green willow sapling. The gooier the better. A tough wet sapling taken from a swampy area would last about a day. This worked well during the dry season, but when the rains came that runner sank in the muck. After jacking that Fordson up level three times in one morning's plowing, Nels' eldest unbolted the contraption from the spokes of that steel wheel and pitched it over the wood-lot fence where parts of it may still be resting today. In defeat, there was a victory for the implement dealer who was always so happy to see him when he came in for more wheel bearings.

As you sidled along the four-cylinder engine block, you noticed something unconventional. It was a cast-iron tank of about two gallon capacity with two-inch threaded plugs top and bottom that only a large hex-end wrench that came with the tractor would fit. It was attached to a flange at the point where the transmission was bolted to the engine block. It was called an air washer. Air consumed by the engine was bubbled through this water. The operator was asked to claw the mud out of this tank and refill it with clean water each day when working in dusty conditions. It was good for something. A kid could grab that big air-washer wrench, release the water, curl his small hand up in that hole and come out with a handful of the best clay marble makings available anywhere. A country kid could go to town come Saturday, if he was just a fair shooter with a half dozen homemade clays, and clean those city slickers out of all their "glassies." The intent of this air cleaner was also good, but much abrasive dust went right on through to the combustion chambers. It did not tarry long enough in the vicinity of the water and the dust survived by staying in the middle of the bubble. After a few hundred hours, the piston slap would be so loud when you started a cold engine you would think you had thrown a rod.

The early Fordson had a bad habit of getting hot, stalling, flooding over at a weak spot somewhere along the gas line and catching on fire. Oh, for a Ralph Nader in those days. The fuel-delivery components were of brass, copper and solder. That solder was the weak link. It did not take much heat to soften it and the engine vibration would do the rest. That engine was not set in a cradle, on springs, rubber or any other type of suspension. It was one contiguous hunk of iron from the ground up. When the fuel system started to break up, you would first get a whiff of gasoline fumes. This would cause you to look around both sides of the engine by straddling the steel seat and standing up on the rear axle housings. You might also check the gas-tank cap to see if it was tight.

This was the proper time to shut her down, but you never did. You always wanted to get to the end of the field or back to the garden where the hired girl had been giving you the eye. You

FROM THE REAR
Fordson, under load, contemplating what it can pull on the driver next.

lifted the plow at the headland and noticed a wisp of white vapor swirling in the area of the red-hot manifold. An instantaneous flash and a puff of black smoke were warnings to flee the vicinity. The power supply to the engine was cut by a disconnected or a severed gravity-fed fuel line. The engine ceased to fire. Flames engulfed the gas tank. The only shutoff valve was a manual brass spigot under the tank right in the center of the hottest of the hot. You the farmer, quickly summarized that there were two choices. First, back off ten rods and let her blow. The other was to take the chance of your life or at least the chance of being severely burned and try to save the grey culprit. The die was cast. Gamble. Yes! With extremely long odds. To gamble that a gasoline fed fire could be extinguished without visible aids at the end of a freshly turned furrow a half mile from nowhere was suicidal. Quick! What are the options? Turn off the super-heated bronze valve under the gas tank that was feeding the fire. With what? A steel rod — a steel fence post — a tree branch with which one could nudge the valve to an off position? A fast look-see in the immediate area drew a zilch. "Nuthin'." Another option was to smother the fire. Again with what? Mud, sod, dirt; ya, and lots of it! Lots of moist loose soil with sod attached. One literally grabs up armfuls of fresh turned dirt and pitches it on the inferno. For a moment the flames hold their own, then grudgingly give what remains of the Fordson back to its master. The resuscitation took all of two days. A first reaction was that someone had salvaged the tractor from a bog. Once you had rescued a S.B. (that stands for not what you think, it's an acronym for stress buggy), you did not hesitate to gamble again. Some drivers were burned. Others could have lost their lives, which was not good. Many S.B.'s were cremated, which was good.

There were unlimited additional hypertension incorporators such as the uncompromising seat, the unshielded red-hot manifold and exhaust pipe, the foot rests, the hitch and the worm gear in that rear end.

There were three forward speeds in the transmission. First was so low that it was seldom used. Second gear did it all. Third was so fast that the S.B. could not be idled down to a safe speed because it would stall. The only places you could shift her over into third were while running across a newly plowed field when pulling nothing or on the heavy sod going downhill in the lane. It could be shifted into third gear on a gravel road but there was no way the driver could keep control. Gravel roads were difficult for steel wheels. These roads were arched in the middle and well-drained with deep ditches. Those S.B.'s would start off with a waltz, glide toward a ditch with a two-step and finish you off with a polka when you landed upside down in the ditch with the steering wheel in your belly. Most drivers skipped the polka routine by jumping clear of the varmint. Those front wheels would stand right up on their narrow center steel ribs and dance to the same tune that the cross-lugged drive wheels were using to claw the high spots. It was a solid hunk of metal and should have clung to the road but it was even contrary to the law of gravity, among other things, and seemed to fly or skitter at Will — sometimes at a Joe or a Harry.

"A hairy who?" asks someone.

We could continue to berate the Fordson to no end but it would not be entirely cricket because all the early small farm power plants were equally deficient. It happened to be the one that was our S.B.

CHAPTER X

POT SHOTS FROM WOLVERINE COUNTRY

T HE CHAPTER HEADING here is the result of this author backing himself into a corner with no place to go. It is a situation reminiscent of a befuddled painter who fresh-coats his exit from a room. This label "Pot Shots" allows me an escape from the dilemma of what to do with a non-conforming group of sketches.

Barbershops

When a country blade went to town and secured the services of a barber to trim his locks, he immediately assumed a higher cultural and intellectual position in his community and especially with the eligible women in his neighborhood.

The barbershop was a man's world. It was the exclusive habitat for the male of the species, both young and old; yet it was a place of business.

A wife or sister might break the door a bit to inquire about the whereabouts of a husband or brother, but that was about as far as they ever went. It was a public place. They could go on in if they wanted to. Somehow, they never did before 1920.

This place of business usually had two rooms. A public room in the front and a semi-private one in the rear where checkers, euchre, tobacco spitting and yarn spinning dominated. It was a safe retreat from demands to hoe in the garden, mow the lawn or help with the housecleaning.

Rarely, would there be a written sign. The proprietor's name would be inconspicuous. Perhaps, the only distinction that set it apart from other establishments was the matter of a bit of paint which cost less than the price of a plug of Mail Pouch Chewing Tobacco. Stripes of red, white and blue could be painted on a corner of the building, on a board suspended over the door, or on a post put into the ground like a hitching post. This became known as a barber's pole and was a sign of the barbershop.

My earliest memories of the barber and his shop were tumultuous. There are only a couple of things I recall. Other happenings, because of their repetitious telling, encroach upon the authenticity of these events.

I remember the barber's chair and my father lifting me upon a board that was laid across the arms. Also, the long buggy ride (horse and buggy, not baby buggy) back home with Mother crying all the way. I understand it was the matter of some golden curls and whether they were to go or not to go, at that time.

There have been some stories passed down about having to call a couple of fellows out of the back room to help hold me down. One, Dan Burnham, never ceased to remind me of the event whenever he felt it was necessary to keep me in line.

The tools of the barber trade were meager and his training less than that.

A sure way of getting a good haircut was to have the barber peel it off down to the skin. There would be no notches. It would be smooth and cool, especially in the good old summertime.

Those hand clippers were hair pullers. If the barber attempted to move them up your neck a wee bit faster than the coordinated movement of the blades would tolerate, "Ouch, he gotcha!"

It wasn't always the barber's fault, though. Sometimes, you the

A WOMAN'S VIEW OF A MAN'S BARBERSHOP

customer, would twitch or try to swat a fly at the wrong moment and you "gotcha" yourself.

Those heavy hand clippers were also attention getters. If a barber had a kid in the chair who kept fidgeting around just because he had gotten some hair down his neck inside his heavy underwear, a rap on the side of the head with the clippers would get his attention and remind him that someone was trying to cut his hair.

The essential equipment of a barbershop would include an imposing hand-lift leather seated chair, a marble shelf, back wall mirror combination with a couple of drawers, straight razors, a razor strop, a couple pair of hand-squeeze clippers, coarse and fine tooth combs, a duster brush full of talcum, bay rum and assorted red and green tonics scented with rose water in prestigious looking bottles.

Haircuts were 25 cents and the barber would brag how many he could run off in an hour, thus by simple calculation making him one of the highest paid people in the community "if'n" he could rope up the customers.

Shaves were 10 cents and this was his bread and butter clientele. Most of the other businessmen in town would come by each morning for a shave, as soon as they could break away from their respective stores after opening up for the day's business. I never could figure out who shaved them with the old style German steel straight razor on Sunday mornings. Each customer for a morning shave would have his individual shaving-soap mug which would help to decorate the shop. Some of those were hand painted with game scenes and others with different types of "wildlife" were turned so the decorative side was not visible to the customers.

A barber would do meticulous work on these regulars with his straight razor, because they paid his rent and gave him an opportunity to develop a camaraderie with his fellow businessmen that was equivalent to a modern day chamber of commerce.

This was still a man's world. Thus, the barbershop was the hub of ideas, the center of activity, and a place for story telling and recreation.

It has always been a familiar institution and a haven for those who enjoyed freedom of speech — relating to gossip, the exchange of opinions and expression of political ideologies. To put it bluntly, it was a great place for a man or boy, because he could go in and shoot off his mouth all he wanted to without offending anyone or getting into trouble.

It was also an example, in early Americana, of the primitive association for businessmen. The barbershop was the location of serious private discussions. Plans were first talked over here on public improvements. Was the sexton doing his job at the cemetery? Would the schoolhouse be needing a new coat of paint this spring? Who could we get to pitch for our ball team so that we could clean up those rascals from the next township come the Fourth of July? Early country and small-town merchants put down their roots in this pattern, and it was good.

Rationing — Voluntary

There are only two kinds of rationing, compulsory and voluntary. Neither are enjoyable. Let's talk about the last one first.

Voluntary rationing, because of necessity, was practiced often by the pioneer families. Never was it more important than during the two winters connected by the summer months of 1816. These months have been labeled by history as the year of no summer.

According to accounts, abnormally low temperatures prevailed and little food for either man or beast was produced. Many almanacs stated that it snowed during every month of 1816 and there were frosts during the summer as far south as New Jersey.

According to the "Farmer's Almanac" many birds dropped dead. Sheep newly shorn, died.

The failure of the corn crop caused extreme hardship and the threat of starvation became a reality. Not only were the people pressed for food but also for seed to put out a crop for the next year. Voluntary rationing was a must, without hoarding. With rationing and by sharing they survived. It was a critical period in the annals of our nation.

The only substantiated scientific fact we recognize that could have caused this severe drop in average temperature during the year of 1816 was a great volcanic eruption. This took place on the

Island of Java, now Indonesia. The disturbance was so large that it encircled the earth with volcanic debris, ash and gases from the subterranean bowels of the earth and changed the weather pattern to the extent that rationing was a necessity. This rationing was voluntary.

Wartime Rationing — Compulsory

During various wartimes it was necessary to ration certain essential goods. This was compulsory.

To secure a permit to buy new transportation during World War II, the recipient had to be working in a defense related occupation. If your mobility was non-essential, new tires were not obtainable.

It was humorous to observe at what lengths ingenious individuals would go with their improvising in attempts to replace tires for automobiles. Junkyards were ransacked by hordes of vehicle owners in need. Farm auctions were watched with eagle eyes for a piece of machinery that might have a useable piece of rubber to fit a particular wheel. I know one character who picked up a piece of large snubbing rope formerly used on a Great Lakes carrier, braided it about a rim and used it for a spare.

It became so bad that few travelers had an extra tire in their trunk. A new generation of panhandlers emerged with a different approach.

A distressed salutation would go something like this, "Mister, do you have a spare?" A purchase order for a tire was difficult to secure. For a spare it was impossible. If you had a dependable piece of rubber on each wheel, you were better off than most motorists.

Should you be blessed with a permit to buy a new auto, there were no choices as to makes, models, options and colors. The lucky one accepted what the dealer had at list price. There was absolutely no wheeling and dealing.

The real tight rationed items were gasoline and meat. Regulations on gas were tolerable. If you played it straight you could get